Grow old along with me!
The best is yet to be,
The last of life. for which the first was made:
Our times are in His hand
Who saith "A whole I planned.
Youth shows but half: trust God: see all nor be afraid."

Robert Browning

RETIRE TO ADVENTURE!

by

Harrison M. Karr

Second Printing 1967
Third Printing 1970

PUBLISHED BY

Trail-R-Club of America

America's Largest Publisher of books pertaining to trailers and mobile home living.

Box 1376   Beverly Hills, California

A PATHFINDER BOOK REPRINT EDITION
Complete and Unabridged

Printed in the United States of America

ISBN: 979-8-8691-7412-3

FOREWORD

Since I retired in 1954 my wife Shirley and I have spent a major part of the time traveling the highways and byways of the United States, Canada, and Mexico in a travel trailer. Always we have been searching for adventure — adventure suitable to our years and physical capacities.

Other adventurers no doubt have faced greater hardships and dangers, and have performed more feats of daring. But not one of them, I feel sure, has derived more downright fun from searching for and finding lively adventure. The following pages recount some of the outstanding events in our eight years of carefree wandering.

If this book succeeds in making some small contribution to the literature on adventure, the contribution will be this: it suggests a mode of adventuring that is available to almost any retired person of reasonably good health and a modicum of financial independence.

The Author

CENTER: Eight-page picture insert—some tangible "memory-pictures" of our happy years of trailering in our own U.S.A., Canada, and Mexico.

Dedicated to the late Wally Byam, bold adventurer and dynamic leader, who showed many thousands of us the way to a rich and full retirement through following the adventure trail.

CHAPTER I

FROM EMPLOYMENT TO UNEMPLOYMENT
IN ONE EASY LESSON

Fortunate is the person who makes the transition from employment to retirement smoothly and easily. Often the change is accompanied by distressful emotional upheavals.

Through a lucky set of circumstances, in my case the transition was marked by a unique, exciting, and highly enjoyable adventure. The circumstances were these: At a Palm Springs trailer rally in the spring of 1954 a Mr. Ulysses (not his real name, but considering his adventurous nature it's a good name) made a speech and showed colored motion pictures of a recent trailer caravan he had conducted to Mexico and Guatemala. Afterward he told of other caravans being planned. To a trailerist on the point of retiring, as I was, this was heady stuff. Later, when I was introduced to Mr. Ulysses, I said:

"Those caravans sound exciting. Sometime I'd like to go on one."

"How about the one to Western Canada starting in June?" he countered.

"Afraid not," I said. "You see, I'm about to retire. I don't know . . ."

I was going to say I wasn't entirely sure how my finances would work out. But Mr. U, an impulsive fellow, broke in.

"When?"

"June."

"Fine," said he. "Just right. Come along."

I decided that I could be as abrupt as he was. On impulse I inquired, "How about my coming along and writing up the caravan for the press—for a little pay?"

"What have you written?"

"I've written two textbooks and . . ."

Without waiting for me to finish the sentence Mr. Ulysses snorted, "Textbooks!" and strode off.

Well, I thought, that ends that. But later that evening while looking through the display of travel trailers including some manufactured by Mr. U's organization, I met some of the people who work for him. Still under the spell of his pictures, I once more expressed the hope that sometime I might go on one of his big adventures. I was of course giving expression to one of those vague *sometimes* that make up so much of our thinking and dreaming. The whole idea of going on a trailer caravan was still pretty much of a dream.

My wife Shirley and I had been trailerists for a number of years, using our little travel trailer to go here and there to points of interest during my vacations. But a trailer caravan—going on a six- or eight-week excursion to a foreign country in company with an aggregation of other trailerists—that was something else. Fun maybe, an exciting adventure undoubtedly, but . . . well, we'd think it over and do some financial planning and perhaps sometime . . .

Shirley was the only one at home when the phone rang—this was several weeks after the trailer assembly. The call was from Mr. U's secretary. After some preliminary amenities, she said:

"We've just been disappointed by the man who was to drive the caboose on the Western Canada caravan starting next week. Sickness. We . . . ah . . . wondered if you and Mr. Karr wouldn't like to go along in that capacity."

"Caboose . . . ?" said Shirley.

"Yes, you know, bring up the end of the caravan. See that no stragglers are left behind. You'd drive Mr. Ulysses' jeep."

"Jeep?" said Shirley. "Well, I . . ."

"It's a jeep station wagon," interrupted the secretary.

"That sounds better," said Shirley, "but I . . ."

"Mr. Ulysses likes to have it along in case of an emergency. It's equipped with four-wheel drive, compound-low gears, and a winch . . ."

"Oh," exclaimed Shirley, "I don't think Harrison knows much about low compounds and winches and . . . those other things." She knew that as a college professor of speech (at UCLA for the previous quarter century) such machinery was out of my line. She concluded her exclamation with the question, "By the way, just what *is* a winch?"

"A winch," said the secretary, "is a . . . it's a . . . Oh, never mind. Mr. Ulysses will explain it. Anyway you and Mr. Karr wouldn't be expected to *use* it. You'd have it along, well, just in case. If the need arose Mr. Ulysses or one of the other men accustomed to such things would use it."

In that remark the secretary told a whopper. But she didn't intend to. And, anyway, the fact that I did have to use some of the equipment gave me one of my all-time big moments. But I'm getting ahead of my story. More about that later.

As a clincher the secretary concluded with, "We have a fine new trailer for you to use. And Mr. Ulysses will pay all your gasoline and other car expenses. You and Mr. Karr think it over and let us know."

When I got home and heard the news I was excited. That matter of car expenses pulled a lot of weight. About to go on a restricted diet, financially speaking, expenses weighed heavy in our thinking. With car expenses provided for, one big obstacle to going on a caravan was removed. But I didn't have much hope. Shirley is a musician, not a golfer, swimmer, or mountain climber. In fact she's not the outdoor type at all. I had felt lucky when I got her to take up trailering, and profoundly grateful when she had come to like it as much as I did. But the thought of her tagging along with me in a jeep, even if it was a station wagon, behind a whole battalion of trailers—the secretary had told her that sixty-some already had signed up and more names were coming in all the time—I couldn't see her doing it. For that matter, neither could she. She said so with emphasis.

And to tell the truth, although I didn't admit it to Shirley, I had trouble getting the picture of myself as the transporter and guardian of all that paraphernalia, even if I didn't have to use the stuff. But I was eager to tackle it. Whatever deficiencies the setup had, it was far more inviting than drifting aimlessly into the worrisome period of transition from employment to unemployment. But, as I say, from Shirley's reaction I felt that the deal was hopeless.

At that point, however, I got an assist from the family doctor—who happened to be our son. That evening at his home, after his wife had put the children to bed and we could hear ourselves talk, I told him of the invitation. His response was immediate and positive.

"Why, that's great, Dad! What a wonderful way for you to start retirement! To tell the truth, I've been worried about you, the next few weeks that is, while you are getting used to no job." Then, noticing the expression on my face, he added, "You're certainly going to accept the offer, aren't you?"

"Talk to your mother," I said.

"Mom," he said, "your doctor says for you to *go!* Doctor's orders, you know . . ."

That was how it came about that one week I was listening to student speeches at the University of California and the next week I was driving across country in a small, compact, somewhat phlegmatic jeep station wagon carrying equipment with which I was hardly on speaking terms. We were on our way to Glacier National Park in Montana, where the caravan was to assemble. The jeep had had some rather hard usage on previous caravans—hauling a half-hundred cars and trailers across a bridgeless river in Guatemala, and similar feats of strength and endurance—and showed its years.

The paraphernalia consisted of four-wheel drive, compound low gears, altimeter, compass, shovels, axes, ropes, cables, and of course the winch. All of this stuff bothered me a good deal. I felt like the Connecticut Yankee in King Arthur's Court, accoutered with a heavy set of armor that didn't fit me.

Besides the machinery there were other things that gave me concern. On the long slow trip we had plenty of time to ponder them. What kind of people went on these caravans? What about regimentation? One thing about trailering that we particularly enjoyed was the freedom to come and go without regard to anybody's wishes but our own. No worry over room reservations, time schedules, or any other of the customary bothersome details associated with traveling.

And here we were starting out on a long hegira with a gang of people we didn't even know. Would we have to "knuckle under" to the wishes of a bunch of strangers? Just what had we let ourselves in for? In particular, just what had *I* let myself in for with all that machinery? Well, we'd just have to wait and see.

We were nearly a week out of Los Angeles when we finally pulled into the caravan's campground on the shore of St. Mary's Lake in Glacier Park. We arrived as the sun was dropping toward the mountain peaks to the west. The huge aggregation of trailers— ninety-three of them — was arranged in a series of concentric circles, after the custom of the Forty-niners on the plains. In the center was a hum of activity. Tables were set for an outdoor meal and people were beginning to sit down. As we approached, a man detached himself from the group and came over to us. He introduced himself as chairman of the parking committee.

"I'll help you get parked," he said. "Then come to supper. We're having potluck."

"Oh, we couldn't," Shirley protested. "Not tonight. I haven't a thing ready to bring."

"Bring your appetites. That's all you'll need ... Here, let me introduce you to some of these people. I'll take care of your rig while you get acquainted."

He led us to a couple of vacant chairs, introduced us to our table mates, and as he left, admonished, "Dig in! Don't be bashful. There's plenty, you'll see."

And there was plenty, no question about that. And there was no question about the heartiness of our welcome. There was an air of conviviality all around us suggestive of a big family reunion at a picnic. And in a sense it was a reunion, for many of these people, we learned, had been on previous caravans together. They were greeting each other like long-lost brothers and sisters. But the fact that we were new did not exclude us from the sociability, nor from the festivities that followed the meal.

After supper a huge bonfire was lighted. Someone sang out, "Any musical instruments in the crowd?"

A slender middle-aged man whom everybody called Bill—later identified as Bill Martin—went to his trailer and brought out a violin which he began to tune. When no one else volunteered, Shirley mustered her courage and said, "I have a small electric organ, if someone can provide the electricity."

"Fetch it out," commanded a big, jovial, farmerish-looking fellow near us. "I got a light plant on my truck. Plenty of juice."

The little electric organ that Shirley brought out was one that we always carry with us. The manufacturer really intended it for a toy— an expensive toy. It is no bigger than a typewriter. Shirley can carry it around as easily as I carry my typewriter. But it has two octaves of true tones of considerable volume—achieved by a wind bellows. By clever manipulation of the tiny keys Shirley can play many of the best-loved old familiar tunes. Together she and Bill Martin accompanied us while we sang *The Old Mill Stream, Darling Nellie Gray, Sweet Adeline*, and so on down the line.

When our windpipes got tired someone called out, "How about square dancing? Anybody who can call?"

"Ah reckon ah could do that," came a soft Southern drawl. A tall, spruce-looking Southerner stepped forward. He was, we learned, a chiropractor from South Carolina on a prolonged vacation. He had already been in camp several days while the caravan was assembling and evidently had established himself as quite a favorite.

"Good for you, Doc Joe," somebody yelled. "Git goin'."

Doc Joe had an engaging grin and a warm, friendly voice to go with the grin. Shortly he had us all dancing a square dance. We had to watch our step because of the gopher and prairie dog holes. But we were stepping high, wide, and handsome, and the rough ground didn't matter.

Early the next morning a lusty voice came vibrating through the walls of our trailer. Looking out we saw Mr. Ulysses calling through a megaphone.

"Meeting time! Meeting time!"

A centripetal movement of trailerists carrying folding chairs, a semi-circle arrangement of chairs around Mr. Ulysses, and the meeting began.

"Everybody stand up and give his name, home town, and line of business. You start us off," said Mr. Ulysses, pointing.

The "You" were a man and wife from Maine. And as we went the rounds it seemed that most of the states of the Union, as well as three or four Canadian provinces, were represented. And when it came to announcing occupations, I got the answer to one of my questions, "What kind of people . . .?"

There were all kinds: the butcher, the baker, and the—electric light manufacturer. There were, besides myself, several other teachers. There were plumbers, carpenters, firemen, policemen, and farmers. There were lawyers, doctors (two M.D.'s), and merchants. And there were several women, widows mainly. It was about as heterogeneous a group, occupationally speaking, as you'd be likely to find. One fairly common element, however, was noticeable. That was age. On the whole we were well along in years. The reason: it is usually only retired or semi-retired persons who can take time to go on such long excursions. But even in this particular there was no complete uniformity. One couple in their twenties were on their honeymoon. Several middle-aged couples were on long vacations. And there were quite a number of grandchildren traveling with the grandpapas and grandmamas. A newspaper along our route stated that our ages ranged from eight to eighty—an understatement, for one man accompanying his son and daughter-in-law was well past eighty.

After the introductions came the setting up of committees, which was largely a matter of volunteering. In addition to the parking committee which was already functioning, there was a committee to take charge of mail, one on social activities, one on civic affairs (chiefly to exchange courtesies with local dignitaries in the towns and cities we visited), one on cleanliness and sanitation (one of our M.D.'s headed this committee), and several other committees essential to a democratic society. These committees were, in a large sense, our governing bodies. And there we got the answer to another of our questions, "What about regimentation?" We were accustomed to living in a democratic society where the majority ruled, setting up such regulations as seemed necessary for the well-being of the group. This was no different.

At the last the Karrs were presented as "caboose." Mr. Ulysses considerately announced, "Mr. Karr lays no claim to mechanical skill. He will not be expected to use the equipment he is toting. But he'll have it along, just in case."

Another of those whoppers! Unintentional, of course, but it goes to show you never can be sure. I'll tell you more about that fib when the time comes. In fact, it would be hard to keep me from telling about it.

Blue berets, the distinguishing insignia of the caravaners, were distributed. These when perched on our heads at the rakish angle most of us oldsters affected, made us feel young, Bohemian, and a bit devilish. They also served wherever we went to get us a lot of recognition, and not a few favors.

As we were disbanding Mr. Ulysses sang out, "Just a minute! Just a minute! An important announcement!"

The announcement was that the Canadian border officials were coming to our camp to take care of admission details. The border was twenty or thirty miles away, but they came. One of the trailers was converted into a temporary immigration-customs office, and registration for the entire caravan was taken care of in about an hour. Next morning the crossing of the border consisted of an exchange of smiles and hand waves with the officials, nothing more.

On Canadian soil, we headed for Calgary. On the highway our caravan spread out. This took care of one of my anxieties, an anxiety shared by one of our Los Angeles friends when we told her of our proposed caravan trip.

"Imagine!" she exclaimed. "How'd you like to get hung up on the highway behind a string of seventy-five or a hundred trailers?"

She needn't have worried. We didn't travel "in a string." Our custom was to set the time of meeting at our next destination, then let nature take its course. Some like to get up early, some late. Some like to travel fast, some slowly. There was only one limitation, and that was self-imposed by the group at Mr. Ulysses' suggestion. Out of consideration for other traffic no more than two trailers were ever to travel close together—except when we were convoyed by Royal Mounted Policemen, a courtesy which was extended to us whenever we entered a city and whenever we traveled through rugged or potentially dangerous country.

When Shirley and I are on trailer tours she always keeps a brief account of our doings, sort of a trip log. Her skeletonized account of the next few days' activities reads:

July 1. Leaving for Calgary. Raining. Detour on muddy roads. Arrived in Calgary camp to find parking committee standing in rain and mud. One man told us he had changed clothes three times. Still they were on the job, waiting for our arrival and helping us park. Dominion Day in Canada, all stores closed.

July 2. Sun shining. Great cleaning of muddy cars and trailers. Milk, bread, and ice delivered at trailers. Men using power mowers preparing ground for dancing tonight. (Evening) Doc Joe called for square dancing and taught us some new steps very quickly. Still light at ten o'clock.

July 3. Beautiful sunny day. At morning meeting Genevieve Bailey of Jackson, Michigan, appointed to buy Stampede tickets for all of us. (Our arrival at Calgary had been timed to coincide with the famous Calgary Stampede.) Meeting disturbed by planes overhead; we learned it was aerial photographers taking pictures of our camp. Went shopping. Calgary bubbling with excitement over the Stampede *and* our caravan. Lots of interest in blue berets.

July 4. Big celebration in camp. Mr. Ulysses' birthday. Many guests, including Princess Wapiti, Queen of Stampede, with her mother and her proud-looking father Chief Eaglespeaker dressed in white buckskin suit and feather headdress. Mayor and Chief of Police made short speeches of welcome. Powell River Bagpipe Band in colorful Scottish uniforms marched and played for us. Caravaner Charles Maskell and two volunteer helpers barbecued hamburgers for all the caravaners and all the guests. Some of the trailer ladies had baked birthday cake for Mr. Ulysses; cake decorated with silver trailer on top. Huge success.

July 5. Big parade through city streets. Three trailers included among the many floats. Attended afternoon session of Stampede.

July 6. Attended night session of Stampede. Chuck-wagon races exciting. Stage show and crowning of Princess Wapiti as Queen. Fireworks.

July 7. Off for Banff...

In Banff, the heart of one of America's most scenic wonderlands, our camp was several miles out of town. It was a grassy meadow through which flowed a stream of clear mountain water. The meadow was surrounded by high mountains that thrust their snow-capped peaks proudly into the blue sky. Over all was the hush of the great mountains. In contrast to our many human visitors in Calgary, here our guests were deer and elk that wandered across our green meadow and drank from our clear stream; a bear that appeared silently at the edge of our meadow, took one quick look at us and swiftly and silently disappeared; a flock of white mountain goats that came down from the peaks and looked us over at leisure. In addition to the animals, the chief ranger of the park and some of his staff came to bring maps and literature and to tell us of trips they planned to take us on. At our solicitation they stayed for our evening wiener roast.

One of our days here was spent at the Indian Days celebration. Another day a conducted tour took us for a boat ride on Lake Minnewanka where we saw the mouth of the swirling river upon which the motion picture "The River of No Return" had recently been filmed. Another excursion was to that lovely sleeping lady, Lake Louise, and to the equally lovely lake that nestles in a mountain valley above it, Moraine Lake. But in my opinion the most breath-stopping scenery we saw was on an overnight jaunt to Jasper Park. Snow-capped peaks lined most of our route. At one point we pulled to the side of the road to stare straight up a sheer cliff over which tumbled eight separate waterfalls, streamers of shimmering lace hundreds of feet long. Over the lace two distinct rainbows played. At another point we left the highway for a mile or so to look almost straight down at an opaque green gem called Peto Lake. Again we paused to gaze at the vast expanse of Columbia Ice Fields, an enormous glacier from which rise streams that become mighty rivers to flow to three separate oceans: the Athabasca empties into the Arctic; the Saskatchewan wends its devious way to Hudson Bay and thus into the Atlantic; the Columbia takes off as if it were headed for the North Pole, but after a couple of hundred miles changes its mind and turns back south, ultimately, after traveling more than twelve hundred miles, to empty into the Pacific Ocean far down in the United States.

Finally, on the way home from Jasper the following evening, we were blessed with one of those rare moments of beauty so sublime that even a lavishly generous Mother Nature can afford only one or two such pictures in one man's lifetime. It was late evening but in that north country the sun was just leaving the sky. The sunset painted the snowy mountains a rosy pink. An enormous round yellow moon was rising majestically between the pink mountains and climbing toward the blue above. And then, as we came over the crest of a hill, Bow Lake was spread out before us, holding the pink mountains, the yellow moon, and the blue sky in reflected glory, a double exposure to bring us double delight. We can be thankful that a man's memory retains certain memory-pictures to enrich all of his remaining days.

From the sublime to the ridiculous! The next leg of our journey was over a road so rough that many would consider it ridiculous for a sane person, let alone a whole caravan, to try to negotiate it. One thing about Mr. Ulysses' caravans, he warns you in advance that you're not always going to stick to the beaten paths; sometimes you're going to take to the backwoods. The road from Lake Louise to Golden is a case in point. Judging by the rock formations, Mother Nature must have suffered some terrible convulsions when she gave birth to the area. Not only that, at the time we went through the road was being dynamited in an "improvement" program. Probably the improvement has been completed by now; I haven't been back to see. All I know is, in that summer of 1954 it was a shambles of big and little rock fragments, with a barely passable trail winding through the rocks. Because of the dynamiting, even the snake-like trail was closed during working hours. But due to group planning and Canadian cooperativeness, the blasting was suspended long enough for our caravan to go through. A handsome young Mountie, mounted not on a steed but on a motorcycle, took the lead and we started through. It was early morning, and the clear, crisp mountain air gave a lift to the spirit. It was a wonderful morning for an adventure. And—Shirley and I had it.

It was on this scrambled, topsy-turvy road that this erstwhile professor came the closest he ever had come or probably ever will come to realizing a dormant-since-childhood ambition to perform some heroic deed. Actually, I must admit, there are people who would not look upon my feat as outstandingly valorous. But valor is a matter of spirit, and the professor's spirit says it was terrific. All Shirley's notes say of the affair is, "The Harts (not their real name) had a breakdown and we pulled them for five or six miles—" which only goes to show how a wife can underrate her husband's achievements. Let me fill in the details.

Soon after we left Lake Louise and began the climb toward the pass, long before we reached the bad road, the rest of the caravan left the caboose far behind. Our faithful but phlegmatic jeep was doing the best it could but that wasn't good enough even to keep the other trailers in sight. By the time we came upon the Harts we had no notion of how far ahead the others were; probably miles.

The Harts were stranded in a section called Kicking Horse Pass, and never was a bit of topography more appropriately named. On one side of the trail was a towering cliff. On the other side, in a deep canyon, was Kicking Horse River, looking as if a wild mustang had kicked it into a seething foam. The Harts' station wagon carried four passengers: the Harts, their married daughter, and a granddaughter. Mr. Hart being an ardent fisherman carried his own boat on top of his station wagon, and inside he carried an outboard motor. With their twenty-five-foot trailer (one of the larger trailers in the caravan), the boat and motor, the four passengers and all their personal gear, it was a heavy outfit.

Mr. Hart said his car wouldn't move. He thought his clutch was burned out, or possibly his gears were stripped, or something. He wasn't sure what. And I, knowing my mechanical limitations, didn't offer a peep. It wasn't feasible to rush ahead and try to overtake Mr. Ulysses; our sturdy jeep wasn't good at rushing. But there was, we knew, a time limit on the work suspension. We didn't know how soon blasting would begin again. Mrs. Hart and Shirley looked apprehensively up the canyon, and Mr. Hart and I looked disconsolately at his motor.

The question of the moment was, what should a professor of speech do under such circumstances? Make a speech?

Mr. Hart made the speech. "Do you suppose you could pull us?"

Now Mr. Ulysses had told me how powerful the little jeep was when it was really geared down. He also had emphasized (boasted a little) how ruggedly his trailers were built. "Don't need to worry if you ever have to pull another outfit out of a mess. Just hook 'em right onto your bumper. It'll take it ... Of course," he added, "*you* aren't ever going to have to. But, you know, just in case!"

Well, here was the "just in case." Also it was my moment of truth.

"Sure we can," I said.

"I've got a tow chain somewhere," said Mr. Hart.

While he fished among his tools for a tow chain I fished deep in my memory for the instructions on how to shift into compound low and four-wheel drive. When we both found what we were looking for, we wound his chain around the station wagon's front bumper and our trailer's rear bumper, and away we went. Not very fast, however. In compound low and dragging his heavy outfit, five miles an hour was top speed. But that was fast enough for me. The churning, roaring river far below, seemingly straight down from the edge of our boulder-strewn trail, wasn't conducive to speed. As I took a quick peek down at the seething maelstrom, I drew back with a shudder. "Harrison," I said to myself severely, "how in the *devil* did you ever get yourself into a mess like this?" And I answered myself just as severely, "Harrison, you should have stuck to your speeches."

But everything seemed to be coming along all right. I began to relax. Then I began to feel a glow of pride. Then ... there came a lurch. Our jeep shot ahead at the scary speed of possibly ten miles an hour. At the same time there came a frightened yell from the Harts, somewhere behind. I glanced up the canyon to see if a dynamite blast had gone off, but no rocks were sailing through the air.

Shirley called out, "Oh oh! You've left them behind. The chain broke."

I backed up. Stimulated by visions of dynamite-hurled rocks, Mr. Hart and I searched frantically through the jeep's equipment for a heavier chain. Ropes, pulleys, wrenches, shovels, axes, even fire extinguishers were pushed aside. Finally we came to a logging chain heavy enough to pull a battleship. Again we tied the two rigs together, and again we moved—at our wonted five miles an hour. If you haven't driven at that speed lately you should try it to see how much time it gives you to think—about things like possible dynamite blasts, for instance, and how far down it is to a seething river.

After a long, long, *long* time—perhaps an hour by the clock—we came to a bridge. Men and road-building machinery were standing waiting. A determined-looking foreman stepped forward and dramatically raised a restraining hand.

"No fu'ther!" he commanded. "They told us to hold up work until the caboose come by. You're it, I reckon. But they didn't say nothin' 'bout..." he paused to point an accusing finger at the Harts, and finished the sentence with a jab in their direction, "...them! You gotta leave 'um here!"

"Why!...Why! They're part of the caravan," I sputtered. "You mean just because it wasn't specifically mentioned that we'd be hauling somebody, you're going to... You can't *do* that!"

"I mean because..." he paused again to exercise his flair for the dramatic, pointing at a steep incline in the road immediately beyond the bridge, "you don't have what it takes to haul 'um over *that*."

Looking at the hill ahead I could see the truth of his observation. While I was deliberating what to do, he decided for me.

"We gotta get on with our dynamitin'. You go on ahead."

I shook my head.

"Go on, I tell ye! You c'n send a tow truck out from Golden." The town of Golden lay somewhere up ahead.

When I still hesitated, he relented enough to say, "You don't need to worry. We'll see they don't get hurt."

Reluctantly, and followed by the Harts' rueful glances, we started on.

Then came the Royal Mountie to the rescue. Scarcely had we crossed the bridge before he came roaring back on his motorcycle, bumping over the rocky roadbed.

"What's holding you up?"

We explained the situation. To our relief he took charge.

"You push on," he said. "I'll go over and reassure the Harts. Then I'll head back to Golden and send out the tow rig."

Soon he roared past us on his way to Golden, bumping wildly over the rough road. Before we got to town we met the tow truck headed for the Harts.

It is good to report that Mr. Hart's trouble was less serious than he thought; merely an overheated and badly slipping clutch. He overtook the caravan a day later.

Meanwhile Shirley and I caught up with the group shortly after their evening meal. We'd been all day on our adventure. The group was engaged in their evening meeting, in the little hamlet of Kinbasket far north on the big loop of the Columbia River. The Mountie had brought them the report of what had happened, and evidently had given the caboose a good buildup. For when we drove into the trailer encampment, the trailerists rose in a body and gave us a standing ovation.

That, I claim, was one of the bright and shining moments of my professorial career. Then, to top off the agreeable experience, Mr. Ulysses had a change of heart regarding my writing. When he had a chance he got me to one side and said, "Hope you're keeping notes. I want you to write up the caravan for the press."

While the meeting was still in progress Mr. Sutton, proprietor of the trailer park, also proprietor of the hamlet's lone gasoline station, store, and restaurant, came over to invite us to come to the restaurant out of the evening chill. We accepted with alacrity, for the air was growing colder by the minute. Once inside the big restaurant, the Suttons turned our visit into a gala occasion. At their suggestion, tables and chairs were pushed aside. A battered piano was wheeled into the cleared space. To start the festivities, surprisingly, Mr. and Mrs. Sutton played a piano duet. What their playing lacked in virtuosity was more than made up in rollicking speed and noise. Then came square dancing with the Suttons joining in. Also joining in were the waitresses. Also lumbermen from nearby woods. Also truckers who hauled the logs on the highway—they came to the restaurant to eat but remained to dance. The handsome young Mountie cut a gay figure in his red coat. Doc Joe's soft Southern voice never showed to better advantage than in this strangely mixed, but hilarious company. It was a night to remember.

And so it went. In Revelstoke we were bivouacked beside a clear lake in whose calm waters we could see the tall evergreens of the opposite shore clearly reflected upside down. In Kamloops, to prove that the region's famous Kamloops trout is not a myth, the Chamber of Commerce brought to the city park, where we were encamped as guests of the city, a kitchen-equipped truck, chefs who were masters of the art of trout cooking, an abundant supply of the savory pink-fleshed fish, and a bevy of the city's prettiest girls to wait on us.

In Okanagan Valley four cities along the shore of orchard-bordered, seventy-mile-long Okanagan Lake entertained us.

Vernon citizenry met us at the edge of town and formed a procession in the middle of the street, with their famous girls' bagpipe band in colorful uniforms heading the procession (the girls were good enough entertainers to be invited that year to march in Pasadena's Rose Parade); they led us to the city park and there hosted us to a turkey banquet.

In Kelowna (home of caravaners Dr. Val and Ady St. John) the

Yacht Club took the entire caravan for a yacht ride; and then on the shore of the lake, beside an enormous bonfire, treated us to "roasting ears," hamburgers, wieners, and all the fixings. An impressive ceremony concluded this evening: led by the city's popular song leader, to the accompaniment of a piano atop a truck, we sang in unison *God Save the Queen* (by the Canadians) and *America* (by the caravaners), to the same tune.

Penticton banqueted us aboard a gayly outfitted ancient paddle-wheel steamer; it had been moored to the dock and converted into a restaurant.

In Summerland caravaners Mr. and Mrs. Milne invited us to their packing plant and showered us with evidence of their fruit and vegetable canning skill.

A few days later we arrived at the mighty Fraser River. Following it for many miles, we arrived at Vancouver — which we entered in typical style. Convoyed by Mounties fore and aft we traversed the city at a fast clip, to the caravan's final bivouac in Swedish Park. Our itinerary, according to plan, brought us to the picturesque city at the time of the British Empire Games. We attended the events *en masse*, watching the emissaries of the far-flung British Empire, Black, Brown, and White, parade in their varicolored costumes, then compete in athletic contests.

The caravan's windup was a big potluck dinner. Afterward Doc Joe was called upon to work out some scheme whereby every member of the group could shake hands with every other member. He accomplished the feat by forming us into two lines moving in opposite directions, then ingeniously altering the pattern. There were, to put it simply, warmth and sentiment in those handshakes. Many of us members of the assembly still look upon the group, some eight years later, as the closest-knit "fraternal organization" of our experience.

One reaction to the caravan came from an elderly widower. In a backhanded, negative sort of way he was paying it a compliment when he said, "When you're with a gang like this, life ceases to be a bore."

Shirley and I, fortunately not having been afflicted by the boredom from which he evidently suffered at times, gave a more positive slant to our appraisal of the caravan. It was, we agreed, by all odds our greatest adventure.

As our doctor had said, "What a wonderful way to start retirement!"

CHAPTER II

REHEARSAL FOR RETIREMENT

I once read in the paper of a drunk in Oakland, California, who drove his car in wild recklessness down a street leading to the bay. Plunging through a guard rail he raced pell-mell off the end of the dock and into the ocean, his car turning turtle and pinning him under. By heroic efforts of a rescue squad he was fished out before he suffocated. But what a shock he must have experienced when he hit the cold ocean water. Quite sobering!

Many retirees suffer some such sobering shock when they retire. I encountered such a retiree in the spring of 1954 a few weeks before I retired. Strolling one evening to post a letter at the corner mailbox, I came upon a long stringbean of a fellow sixty or sixty-five years old leaning on the mailbox. He looked questioningly at me as if wondering whether I would go along with a bit of conversation or would give him the big city brush-off. He took the chance.

"Nice evening," he said.

I agreed that it was a nice evening and added my bit to the topic.

"Lovely," I said. "We're pretty lucky here. Have a good many of these beautiful evenings."

That gave him the opening he wanted. Without wasting any more time on small talk he launched into the subject he really wanted to discuss, himself and his problems.

"Guess so," he admitted, "but I'd give every cent I've got if I wasn't here *enjoying* it."

He stressed the word enjoying to show that he was doing anything else but.

"What's wrong with it?" said I, bristling to defend my home town.

"Not a thing, not a thing," he said hastily. "It's just that I wish I wasn't here."

"Where'd you like to be?" I asked, not much caring but willing to let the unhappy fellow unburden himself.

"Right back in St. Louis where I come from, that's where. On my old job. Going to work with the whistle every morning and going home every night dog-tired. That's where I wish I was."

Without further prodding, indeed with a sort of breathless hurry as if fearful that I wouldn't take time to listen, he went on to tell his story — a story which is being duplicated more or less closely all over the country. All his working years he had been employed by one concern. Starting as a shipping clerk he had gradually worked up until toward the end he was "getting a pretty good salary." All the time he and his wife saved and looked forward to the day when he could retire and they could move west to the land of sunshine where their daughter lived, Los Angeles. That was to be the end of the rainbow.

What he did not tell me, but what was easy to see, was this: along with his financial preparation he hadn't done anything to prepare "spiritually." That is, he had done nothing to cultivate interests outside of the job. He had driven posthaste off the end of the work-dock into the cold and cheerless ocean of no job, no routine, no responsibilities, no anything to fill the void when the work ended.

"Clara gets along okay," he said plaintively. "Her and Isobel — that's the daughter — chatter along like a couple of magpies. They go shopping and have a hell of a time. But what's there for me to do? Walk to the mailbox to mail a letter, gawk into the store windows, stroll over to the park and watch some old duffers like me playing checkers. I tried to work up some interest in the game. But it's no go." He sighed dispiritedly. "What I wouldn't give to be back in the old rat race right now!"

That experience was sobering to *me*, just on the point of retiring. I didn't think I'd be like that, but I wasn't absolutely sure I wouldn't be. I doubt if anyone on the threshold of retirement ever is *absolutely* sure.

The reason I did not *think* I'd be like the gentleman of the mailbox was this: we had had a rehearsal of retirement and knew pretty well what we were getting into. A rehearsal isn't quite the same as the real thing, but it helps.

As stated earlier, at the time of my retirement trailer caravans were new to us. Trailer traveling by ourselves, however, was not new. Shirley and I already were, and for several years had been, enthusiastic trailerists.

My first trailer I bought in 1935, paying $50 for it. That wasn't much to pay for a trailer, even in that depression year. But then, it wasn't much of a trailer. It was called a "teardrop." The name, I think, did not come from any lachrymal associations other than its shape, which was something like a teardrop with a tail. I always thought that "hornet" would have been a better name, for a hornet was closer to its shape. It consisted mainly of a bed wide enough for one and one-half persons. By crowding in, Norman my son of high school age and I could sleep in it, sort of. That is, we could once we got into it, but that was quite a trick. You had to stand on the ground and jump, at the same time twisting your backside around and aiming it toward the open door on the trailer's side, hoping you would get through the door and land on the mattress. The mattress took up all the space inside this compartment. There wasn't even room left over for your shoes or your hat; they had to be left somewhere outside. In addition to this "bedroom," there was a kitchen. You got to this by walking around to the back end of the trailer and lifting up the hornet's tail. Underneath were shelves containing a one-burner gasoline stove, cooking and eating utensils, and your "victuals." No matter what the weather, cooking and eating had to be *al fresco.*

Despite the trailer's limitations, Norman and I had some wonderful trout-fishing excursions into the Sierras. And I remember it with considerable affection.

But it didn't make a hit with Shirley. "Uh-uh," she said. "Too much like camping."

That reference had emotional overtones and undertones. When, in 1925, we moved from Indiana to California, we camped all the way out. We came a long route, taking in Yellowstone Park and other spots of interest. The trip took a full month. What with the dirt, the rain, the seemingly unending setting up and taking down camp, and the likewise seemingly unending packing and unpacking of the car, Shirley got her fill of camping. When we arrived in California she made a pronouncement in no uncertain terms. "As far as I'm concerned," she said, "you can sell the camping outfit. I'm through." So when she compared the teardrop to camping, that meant its finish insofar as she was concerned. She never once got inside it.

Years went by. Norman had finished high school and college and had gone away to medical school. Kay, our daughter, was married. And Shirley and I were settling placidly into the second half of middle age. I had sold, long ago, the half-pint trailer and the thought of owning another trailer had become pretty well buried in the debris of sedentary habits.

Imagine my shock when Shirley proposed, "Let's buy a trailer."

She hadn't gone completely daft. As usual she was motivated by a good and sufficient reason. The reason was: our Kay was about to have her first baby.

Kay's husband, Ray, a recently returned veteran, was starting his own business raising minks and foxes in the mountain community of Big Bear Lake, and they were economizing by living in a house of Tom Thumb proportions.

"Kay wants me and she needs me," said Shirley, "but there's no room in their house for me. I couldn't squeeze in edgewise... but you know, Harrison, I believe I have an idea."

"Yeah, what?"

"There's no room *inside* their house but there's oodles of room *outside.*" And then she sprang the big surprise. "Let's buy a house trailer." By this time she had warmed to her idea and was going strong. "We can park the trailer under their pine trees. That way I'll be there to help Kay and you can come up and do some fishing weekends." Just to keep her in the mood of being an advocate for trailering, I started to register a mild protest; but she had thought her argument all the way through. She went on, "We can buy a used trailer and the cost won't be prohibitive. And after we've finished with it we can sell it."

Shirley's scheme worked according to plan, all except one little detail—that about reselling the trailer. By the time summer was over and Kay was back on her feet and Baby Alison was worming her way deeply into Grandpa's and Grandma's hearts, Shirley thought pretty highly of the trailer. But woman-like she made her next suggestion sound as if it were in my interest.

"You've always wanted to get better acquainted with the desert," she said, "Why don't we *keep* the trailer? We can take it down to Palm Springs to one of the trailer parks and spend some of our weekends down there."

I let her persuade me — it wasn't very hard. Since then we've never been without a trailer. And what's more, we never expect to be.

I take little credit for staging my rehearsal for retirement. It was almost forced upon me. I say *almost*. My condition was not quite like that of an elderly neighbor. Ten years ago he suffered a heart attack that made him stop work. He calls the heart attack his blessing in disguise. "By quitting work and coming to the desert," he says, "I've had *ten years* of happy retired living. If it hadn't been for the heart attack I'd either still be at my job in the city, or . . ." He shrugs expressively.

In my case the situation was this: the University has the policy that the teachers and administrators *may* retire at sixty-two; they *must* retire at sixty-seven. I was only sixty — that was in 1949, five years before my actual retirement — but I was mentally and emotionally exhausted. Having dealt with smart and sophisticated young people for almost forty years, I had the feeling that they had extracted most of the good out of me. My affliction, I suppose, was mainly an aggravated attack of "occupational fatigue." At any rate, the next two years, before retirement was permissible, looked long and almost unendurably burdensome. I went to my superior officers to discuss the possibility of premature retirement with, of course, a reduced pension. In all conscience the pension was to be small enough at best, but under the circumstances I was willing to take a reduction.

Because of my years of service, my superior officers offered a compromise: a sick leave for a semester to see if I could get back on my feet.

Naturally, I accepted the offer. That sick leave was my salvation, partly because the vacation recharged my mental and emotional batteries enabling me to go back to work for another five years, but even more because it afforded me that rehearsal for retirement.

Right off the bat, though, we faced a problem: what to do with that four-month layoff in order to get the most out of it. I felt the need of a change of scene. But we couldn't see ourselves taking off on any sort of deluxe tour — not with the possibility of premature retirement, and premature severance from salary checks, lowering over us. Well, one thing, we had been in the desert enough to know it was a pleasant place to spend the winter months. Also we had a little experience with desert trailer parks catering to "senior citizens," and had found them lively and interesting. Furthermore, we had a trailer. What more natural than that we should hie away to the desert? We hied.

It was in the desert, then, that we staged our rehearsal for retirement. You can learn a good deal in a full-scale dress rehearsal. We learned a lot. Some of the more important items I want to pass along. They are:

First. It is smart to retire gradually.

We had opportunity to observe retirees who had pushed themselves to the very last. Now all they could do was sit outside their trailers and bask in the sun. Well, I thought, even that is better than hanging around the scene of their previous employment — like chips in an eddy outside the main current of the river. It has always seemed to me that the most forlorn retired folk I encounter are these "chips" who stay in the vicinity of their previous employment. Pushed aside by the current, floating round and round but not getting anywhere. Long ago I made up my mind that my first act when I retired would be to get far away from the current I was no longer in.

But it wasn't ideal, even in a park catering to retirees, to be physically incapacitated. Those who had good enough "tickers" to permit them to join in the constant round of activities were getting much more enjoyment out of their retirement.

We began to feel sorry for men who work with increasing tensity as they approach the end of their productive years. You can almost see them glancing worriedly at the calendar and muttering, "So little time left! So much to do!" Such men, we decided, should take time out to take an inventory of their friends who have had a similar philosophy. They should note the number who are confined to invalid chairs, asylums, and cemeteries. All too often the eager beavers who work so frantically to achieve financial security and comfort fail to live very long to enjoy the fruits of their frenetic preparations. They may succeed only in becoming "the richest people in the cemetery." As a result of our observations we concluded that the risks are too great; the potential rewards aren't worth the sacrifice.

In contrast, there in the trailer park we met many who were approaching retirement more sensibly. Learning to retire gradually. Letting go of their workloads a little at a time. And, of tremendous importance, looking for interests with which to fill the approaching void.

Typical of this latter class was a lawyer from Long Beach. He had taken in a junior partner with the agreement that the younger man was to do more than half of the work, leaving the older man free to get away for frequent jaunts to the desert. The arrangement was, naturally, a bonanza for the younger man — thus to step into a well-paying partnership. And it was proving to be a lifesaver for the older man.

Another acquaintance was the owner of a prosperous gasoline station. Gradually, some years previously, he had begun to turn more and more of the management of the business over to his son and son-in-law. He and his wife, meanwhile, had a large mobile home in the desert where they spent frequent weekends, occasional weekdays, and sometimes whole weeks.

About this time we heard from our old friends the Joe Wilsons, long-time trailerists, who in the dim distant past had taken us on our very first trailer trip. Joe had begun to turn his Detroit teacher-placement bureau over to his employees to run a few months each winter — the agency's slack period. The Wilsons, meanwhile, were coming to the Arizona desert. While in the desert Joe was occupying his time by building a house, with his own hands. Joe was immensely happy, satisfying an urge to build. Now, in 1962, as I write this, Joe and Lenore, his wife, are living pridefully in the house that Joe built.

In the park were a dentist, a rancher, a real estate broker, and a high school teacher, all of whom were spending part of their time, long or short periods as occasions permitted, in desert trailers. They were *gradually* adjusting themselves to the post-work way of life. The high school teacher said, "Even if I only come down on Saturday mornings and go back Sunday nights, I get away from my work and worries for a while. It's like taking miniature vacations. I go home refreshed, able to do a better job."

Second. Retired persons can live cheaper than employed persons.

Our rehearsal gave us a new financial perspective. As stated earlier, it enabled me to work five years longer, thus giving my pension a shot in the arm. But more important, we learned that we could live on considerably less than we had been spending. Simpler clothing, low rent, free home-made entertainment, made living surprisingly cheap.

Of necessity, finances have always played an important part in our calculations. But I would not have it appear that this was the case with all the retirees in the park. No indeed! A visitor jokingly inquired, "Is it true what they say, that the poor people in the park wash their own Cadillacs?"

Some of our neighbors in the park made annual trips to Europe. Not a few owned houses elsewhere and lived in the trailer park solely through preference. One retiree, owner of not one but a whole string of stores, said he and his wife "got tired of keeping up a big house just for the servants." For space in some of the swankier parks, particularly those overlooking the blue Pacific Ocean, rentals are so "horrible and awfu'," as Bobby Burns would have put it, that "ev'n to name would be unlawfu'."

There were then in 1949, there are even more so today, many very expensive menages in trailer parks. (Nowadays the preferred term is *Mobile Home Park*. Not wishing to offend mobile home owners, mobile home park owners, or Mobile Home Manufacturers' Association, I'll try to remember to use the preferred term hereafter, even though I'm thinking principally back to 1949 when we spoke freely and unashamedly of our *trailer park*.) Perhaps along the line of expensive setups, it will be enough to say that Bing Crosby, Art Linkletter, and others in their financial bracket are investors in mobile home parks.

But to get back to my main theme, it was encouraging to us to learn how reasonably a person *may* live in a mobile home park, and without being relegated to the other side of the tracks. I will not say that we were entirely free from pressure to keep up with the Joneses. But I *will* say that we felt it less than anywhere else we ever lived.

Third. Retired persons can be happy.

That does not mean simply being free from unhappiness. It means positive, exuberant happiness.

I once heard a university president regretfully say, "I never learned how to play." He was advising the students to enjoy their youth, not to lose the spirit of play. My observation is that most students do not need the advice. But a great many older people *do* need it.

In mobile home parks the spirit of play is cultivated. Swimming pools, shuffleboard courts, square dancing (and in a few parks nowadays golf courses), appeal to the more active. Cards, television, sightseeing trips, and potluck dinners appeal to the more sedentary. And classes in sewing and knitting, metal work, picture-taking, conversational Spanish and other subjects are in sufficient variety to appeal to almost any taste. And, oh yes, one thing more I must not leave out. That's fishing. A host of retirees go fishing. From our park they went to the Colorado River, the ocean, and lakes, streams and rivers far and near. Some had really taken up fishing in a big way. And all seemed to be learning the wisdom of the Persian proverb, "Allah does not deduct from a man's span of years the time he spends in fishing."

It does seem that trailers attract to themselves a special breed of folk. I suppose not everyone is adapted to the way of life. But those who are attracted appear to have a special yen for getting fun out of life. For Shirley and me it was a heartening experience to find so many senior citizens actively engaged in the pursuit of happiness, and finding it!

Let me give you a quick introduction to some of the people there in the park who seemed to us to be getting an extra full measure of fun out of living.

The park fix-it man lived in a trailer in the park. He was fat and jolly; also he was an efficient, clever repair man. Everybody called him Dad. It didn't matter whether you needed plumbing or electrical connections worked over, a storage room built, or a section of your trailer rebuilt, Dad could do it and do it acceptably. There was only one fault. He loved to talk. While he would be working on a job residents of the park would come and ask his advice upon some project or another they would be working on. Dad always took time to advise what should be done and to explain the procedure in detail. At the drop of a chance remark, Dad would say, "That reminds me," and off he would go on a tale, a tale always touched with humor. Naturally, these interruptions slowed down his rate of production. But in the main the park residents took the interruptions in good spirit — partly because Dad worked for ridiculously low wages.

Dad wore on his head a helmet made of compressed paper. When park residents came to borrow tools, which they frequently did, Dad would make a note of the loan on his hat. He explained, "I used to loan tools right and left, without keeping any record. But pretty soon I woke to the fact that I didn't have many tools left. That wasn't right. So I started my bookkeeping system. Only trouble is, gotta buy a new file pretty soon. This one's getting full."

Once when he was working for us, in response to some chance remark he removed his helmet, wiped his forehead, and said, "That reminds me of one time I had to fix one of those sink-and-refrigerator combinations. The quarters were so tight I couldn't get in edgewise. Couldn't even get my head and hands in at the same time. Had to do everything by feel. And when a fellow don't feel so good, it makes it bad."

Another time I heard him explain how he took up trailering and came to the desert.

"You see," he said, "I used to play the tuba. That's what makes me so big here (jiggling his stomach). Wind."

Somebody interrupted. "What's a tuba got to do with trailering, Dad? Neighbors make you move out?"

"No. Not that. I played in the band. One late fall day we had to play at a football game. You know it gets cold back in New England. Cold that day. Close to zero. Well, sir, got my tongue stuck to the metal and couldn't pull it loose. Like to pulled my tongue out by the roots. When I finally did get it off it pulled a square inch of skin off my tongue. Figured it was time to move to a warmer climate."

As I say, nearly everyone in the park accepted Dad as he was and didn't try to change him or his work habits. But one time a newcomer became fidgety over the interruptions while Dad was working for him. Finally when Dad started one of his that-reminds-me's, the man broke in. "Just a minute. Is this yarn on your time or on mine?" With perfect equanimity Dad replied, "On yours, of course." "Then I don't want to hear it," said the man. Not in the least perturbed Dad continued with his anecdote. When he had finished he turned to the man and said, "Take it easy, mister. You'll get your money's worth. Why do you think I work for $.90 an hour when others are getting twice as much and more? So I can have time to talk and be friendly, that's why. Folks that don't have time for that have no business living in a trailer park." And Dad went right on with his that-reminds-me's.

Another resident who afforded us pleasure was the park storekeeper. In the cramped quarters back of the counter, on a high stool, Mr. Farmer, as we'll call him, sat and waited for customers. When they came he greeted them with a hearty warmth that was designed to, and did, bring them back again and again. Like others in the park Shirley and I patronized his market regularly even though we often paid a little higher than we could buy the groceries elsewhere. Mr. Farmer could not always compete on a penny for penny basis with the chain stores. But he gave something that they couldn't: a personal interest in *you*, and a bonus of friendly good humor.

Early one January morning when I went to the market for a newspaper, I was wearing a light topcoat. Mr. Farmer as always greeted me in his strong, hearty, friendly voice. Then he lowered his voice to a near whisper. "Let me give you a little advice," he said. "You're a newcomer here and will have to learn these things. Don't let the Chamber of Commerce people see you wearing that overcoat. They'll ostracize you right out of town. They'll say you're slandering the climate."

Another time I heard him engage in a bit of banter with a woman who was visiting her sister in the park. Mr. Farmer asked her, "Is your husband here with you?" "No," she replied, "I left him at home." "That's safer," said Mr. Farmer solemnly, "with all these grass widows around here competition is pretty keen."

But I guess the funniest piece of foolery I heard him engage in was recounting his experience in raising rabbits. "Had it pretty soft for a while, till competition learned of the racket and cut in on me. Sold the meat to the butchers, the hides to a mail-order house to make mink coats out of, the feet to a watch-fob maker to make good-luck charms, the guts to a hog farmer, the heads to a fox farmer, and the droppings to a nursery. Once I sold a hundred female rabbits to a hospital. They had to be virgins. You wouldn't think a hospital would care about the rabbits' morals, would you? But they did. Had to be virgins. They said they used them to tell whether or not a woman was pregnant. I suppose it was by comparing their facial expressions, the look of innocence in their eyes."

Another time, soon after we went to the park he explained to me why he had been taking on some weight lately. "Just too lazy to get out and exercise," he said.

But I got the real reason for the weight-gaining and also for the constant sitting on the high stool back of the counter the first time I saw him walk. It really wasn't a walk at all. It was a shuffle on crutches, the crutches that he always kept carefully out of sight when they were not in use. His legs, twisted and shriveled from arthritis (the thing that had brought him to the desert) were all but useless.

Altogether, during that period in the trailer park while we were having our rehearsal, Shirley and I heard more laughter—not the laughter that comes in bottles at so much a fifth, but real fun-laughter —than we had heard in years.

Fourth. Successful retirement belongs to those who prepare for it.

A tragic phase of our modern living is that we devote so little thought to preparing for leisure, and consequently use our leisure so foolishly.

The good things of life that come our way don't often just happen. Usually they have to be planned for and worked for.

We became convinced that preparation for *unemployment* in our later years is fully as important as preparation for *employment* in our early years. And, like Robert Louis Stevenson, we concluded that to sow hurry and reap indigestion was not the way to prepare—especially as we get along toward the end of the course.

In the park we met many persons who were reaping the rewards of having prepared for retirement—prepared in mind and spirit as well as in the pocketbook.

When we first went to the park it appeared to us that everybody was devoting full time to rest and play. For a while that suited us perfectly. But when we became rested and rejuvenated a bit we began to realize that for us it wasn't enough. And furthermore, as we got better acquainted we learned that for many others in the park play and rest, rest and play, were not enough. Many had well-developed interests that they actively pursued.

To be sure, there were many who apparently found complete satisfaction in the various types of organized and spontaneous play available: the twice-weekly sessions of square dancing (one for practice and one a dress-up party), the shuffleboard courts (spontaneous games within the park membership and scheduled competitive games with other parks), quoits, checkers, cards, the frequent potluck dinners; and the constant round of fun-activities of many varieties.

But in the park, as well as in social activities outside of the park, it became apparent that the happier people were those who had hobbies. And the very happiest of all were those whose hobbies had been with them for an appreciable period of time, persons who had started their hobbies while they were still actively employed and had carried the hobbies into retirement with them.

An example: One of our closest neighbors was a retired doctor. During his active years he cultivated the hobby of picture-taking; and when he went into it he did it as he did everything, with his whole soul. He studied cameras, picture composition, light values, and the other features that make the difference between good photography and mediocre photography. He used his hobby to get him into the out-of-doors and away from his busy practice (if more doctors were as wise, the medical profession might cease to be the one of shortest mortality). He studied nature and photographed it in many aspects. Now that he was retired his hobby had burgeoned into something extremely worthwhile. He had built next to his trailer a little room with windows that opened wide. Outside, under a mesquite tree, he had erected a bird-bath and a bird-feeding station. Inside the room he had his camera ready on a tripod, with the lens trained on the bird rendezvous. Mockingbirds, finches, bluebirds, and all the other dozens of varieties of birds that make bright and cheerful this section of the desert, came to accept his hospitality, sing their songs of gratitude, and unknowingly pose for the doctor's pictures. Not only was he getting pictures of professional excellence, at the same time he was cultivating delightful bird friendships. Once when Shirley and I went to call on the doctor and his wife, and were sitting on the porch in front of their trailer, a bouncy little rock wren which (I was tempted to say *who*) lived in the mesquite tree, came and lit on the doctor's hand. From a little box which he kept close at hand the doctor extracted a pinch of ground peanuts. Fondly he watched as the tiny bird ate fearlessly from the palm of his hand. Needless to say, time did not hang heavy on the doctor's hands.

One grand couple whom we have come to look upon as among our closest friends had then, and still do have, so many hobbies that the days are not long enough. For one thing, they carried with them into retirement a love of reading, not simply haphazard "escape" reading, but carefully selected books to give them more abiding pleasure. They also carried with them their active interest in civic affairs, and they continue to work for community betterment. When they take their little travel trailer (not the trailer they live in) on short excursions, they prepare. They use the library to read up on the districts they plan to visit. They go to the chambers of commerce and learn the points of interest, and read the literature about the places. Thus they are learning the inside story of many communities and are coming to know the history of our West in an intimate, inside fashion. And they are having a whale of a good time doing it.

One couple have begun the study of stars, a fascinating hobby when you perceive the sparkling brilliance of desert stars.

Among our friends in the park were rock-hounds, bird-watchers, jewelry-makers, camera-enthusiasts, and mountain-climbers. Yes *sir!* we did too have mountain climbers among our elderly residents.

One man in particular, whose brown skin and muscular torso reminded you of an elderly Tarzan, did a stint of mountain climbing every morning before breakfast.

These are not the types of hobbies one picks up today and drops tomorrow. Presumably many of them had been cultivated years back and were carried along into retirement.

As I write this chapter I have before me a page from the brochure issued by the Standard Oil Company of California to its advisers in their extensive program of *Planning Ahead for Retirement*—the title of the brochure. A paragraph from the foreword says:

Experience shows that most people are not sufficiently prepared for the many adjustments necessary for a happy and successful retirement. Preparation for retirement involves a special form of education, and it is hoped that this program will adequately fill the need.

Stimulating interest in forming trailer clubs is one facet of the California Standard Oil Company's program of aiding employees to retire sucessfully.

If there is one single bit of advice, valuable above all others, that we would like to pass along as a result of our rehearsal for retirement, it is this: Do not, above all else, do *not* plunge into retirement "cold turkey." Retirement *can* be a joyous period of your life; do not spoil it by jumping or falling into it unprepared.

Profiting by what we learned in our rehearsal, the first thing I did when I got back into harness was to lop off a part-time job. Some years previously I had been flattered by being invited to assume a part-time administrative post. The work consisted of visiting high school principals and reporting on the success of their graduates in the university—with the objective of aiding in smoothing out the difficult process of changing from high school to university. It was interesting work and I looked upon it as a worthwhile service. I also looked most kindly upon the extra pay. But, added to my teaching, it was taking a good deal out of me. I had looked upon this extra income as essential financial preparation for retirement. But with the truer perspective I had gained in my rehearsal, I realized that compared to the preservation of my health it wasn't so essential after all. The outside job had to go.

The next thing was for Shirley and me to make a solemn resolve not to neglect our "miniature vacations." We had been neglecting them—possibly one reason for my enforced sick leave. That resolve we adhered to. From then on, with religious dedication to the cause of health, we took weekend trips to our trailer home in the desert.

The weekends, I must admit, did not always work out as planned. When I took student papers along to mark, or important material to read, I often suffered distractions. Occasionally the distractions came from friendly neighbors who wanted to visit. But not often. Trailer folk we found to be remarkably considerate of other people's interests. Usually the distractions came from the desert—such as a flock of desert quail crossing my neighbor's yard; he feeds them and they come in droves to partake of his bounty. And, sitting in comfort in the shade of an overhanging mesquite tree, I found it difficult to keep my eyes from wandering off across the desert landscape. However, although I didn't always get my self-imposed quota of work done, I did, as the high school teacher said, go back to the city refreshed, better able to do my job of teaching.

Like most folk, it took Shirley and me some time to develop our present high regard for the desert. At first we came solely for health reasons: to partake of the sunshine, dry air, and clean pure mountain water to drink. But gradually the lure of the desert took hold of us: the dazzling sunshine, the lavishly painted evening skies, the brilliant stars in velvety black night skies, the breath-taking sunrises, the feeling of expansiveness with your eyes looking off to far horizons. Before long the desert had us completely under its spell. We *knew* that for us a part of every year would be spent in the desert. And now, as I write this after eight years of retirement, that is how it is working out.

That matter of knowing where you want to live is one of the greatest potential benefits of a rehearsal for retirement. I am thinking of two retired couples, both of whom dropped into communities where they *thought* they wanted to live. Both couples bought building lots. In each case, before the couple got their house finished they discovered they had made a mistake in their choice of location. One couple was able to sell out. The other couple is still holding the property hoping to sell. A full-scale dress rehearsal gives opportunity to try a community out—materially reducing the chance of making a mistake.

A retired gentleman whom I met on the golf course (one of the pleasant features of retirement is the opportunity to play as much golf as you wish, or can afford, without feeling guilty about wasting the time) was formerly employed by the California Standard Oil Company as an adviser on problems of retirement—the man who let me see the prospectus from which I quoted earlier. He divides persons on the threshold of retirement into four classes: (1) those who want to continue working and more or less bitterly resent compulsory retirement, (2) those who have made no plans, cultivated no hobbies, and simply drift with the tide into retirement, (3) those who look forward to sitting on their porches and watching the rest of the world go by—thereby shortening their lives and inviting the worst kind of ennui, and (4) the few who carefully prepare for retirement so they actually may do the things they have always dreamed of doing—thereby laying the foundation for active, happy retirement.

This grouping suggests that possibly in the neighborhood of one-fourth of our retirees succeed in achieving a wholly satisfactory retirement. I suspect that the percentage is not far out of line. Certainly most people appear to approach retirement quite unprepared in their minds, spirits, and habits.

Considering all that may be learned from a full-scale rehearsal, it would seem to be the part of wisdom if at all possible to stage such a rehearsal. And to do it voluntarily, not waiting as I did till I *had* to stage one.

The next few chapters will recount some of our adventures while I was still employed—part of our program of gradual retirement.

CHAPTER III

AT HOME ON THE OPEN ROAD

All morning we had been traveling along the Redwood Highway, headed north. Hooked on behind was our new travel trailer — new to us, but a slightly used one we had bought at an attractive price. Anticipating more and more trailering, we had sold that first trailer, the one we had taken to Palm Springs earlier. We considered that one to be too big and unwieldly for the open road that was beckoning us. This one was only sixteen feet long. It traveled like a dream.

We were not talking much. As nature's more majestic creations — the ocean at sunset, the sky on a starry night, the great canyon of the Colorado River when filling with evening's purple shadows, and so forth — are likely to do, these giant trees, the oldest and largest of nature's living organisms, had worked their spell on us. We felt humble. And we were quiet.

At the same time we were relaxed and comfortable. We weren't hurrying. No need to hurry. We didn't have to wire or phone ahead for sleeping accommodations; we had them with us. We didn't have to hurry to get to some certain city or town at mealtime; I had one of the best chefs right along with me, and her own kitchen to cook in.

Besides, we were even more relaxed than usual because we had a long vacation ahead of us. No responsibilities for three whole months. I was still employed, but I was taking the entire summer off. For the first time in my teaching career I was going on a prolonged loafing spree. Young professors use their summer vacations to go back to the university to take more courses, get more education. Older professors use the time to work on research projects, to write books, or to teach summer school. But this year, profiting by what I had learned in "our rehearsal," I was just going to play, all summer long. The months stretched out invitingly ahead of us.

In this relaxed — but rather solemn — mood, just at noon we pulled into Williams Grove of Big Trees. We found our way to one of the picnic areas. Immediately we noted an air of excitement among the surrounding picnickers. They were bolting their meals, tossing their dishes and food remnants into baskets, and rushing off.

"What's up?" I called to a family at a neighboring table.

"Motion picture company shooting a picture," the man of the family replied. "*Valley of the Giants.* Just over the hill yonder." And he turned back to his hurried eating.

In and around Los Angeles, during the many years we had lived there, we had seen numerous motion picture companies shooting pictures. Had at times seen them shoot the same scene over and over, and over and OVER, in seemingly endless monotony. So this news didn't thrill us. Anyway excitement wasn't what we wanted from the Redwoods. We wanted peaceful quiet. We drove deeper into the forest to another picnic area. Here was the all-pervading hush which to us is one of the most satisfying characteristics of these silent giants.

We selected a table where welcome sunlight filtered through the lofty trees — welcome because here in the almost perpetual shade even at midday on this bright mid-June day the air was chilly. I switched on the bottled gas. Shirley put the teakettle on to boil, and began the preparation of our simple lunch — the kind of meal we like at noon; not the kind of meal you get in so many restaurants along the highways: the heavy meat, boiled potatoes (usually cold), gravy (ugh!), stewed tomatoes with the tomatoes' life blood soaked up by bread chunks.

She handed things out of the trailer door and I set them on the picnic table: oilcloth table cover, dishes, silverware, bread and butter, lettuce and tomatoes, salad dressing, pickles, a plate of cheese, and the good hot tea. Simple ingredients that Shirley could get easily and that wouldn't leave us stuffed like a miser's pocketbook afterward.

We had just started to eat when company arrived. They were uninvited but I can't say they were unwelcome. There were three of them, three bluejays that took their perches close to our table on the branches of a slender oak sapling which was struggling for existence under the big trees. When we didn't immediately offer food, the guests expressed their opinion of us in pretty strong bird language. "What the blankety-blank kind of hospitality is this? Where are your manners?" they squawked.

When they still got no response, one of them, bolder than the others, hopped down onto the end of our table. He cocked one eye at us and then the other, and yelled, "Why, you d . . . !"

I interrupted his diatribe by rolling a morsel of cheese along the table toward him. He hopped forward, seized the cheese in his bill, gulped, and squawked, "That's more like it. Let's have some more."

Not wanting to show partiality, I turned my back on him and tossed a bit of cheese toward the other two guests. They swooped, but they didn't get it. Our number one bird got it by swooping faster.

"Hey!" said Shirley, "quit wasting my cheese."

"That's for the birds," I quipped. "I'm doing this in the interest of science." And in a sense I was. I wanted to see how much cheese one greedy bluejay could handle.

After lunch I took one of my ten- or fifteen-minute naps, and as usual Shirley got her relaxation from doing a stint of knitting.

That was the first of a whole series of picnics that lasted from Los Angeles into Canada and back, with many side trips. The weather, fortunately, was near perfect most of the time. So we ate most of our noon meals and some of our evening meals outdoors. When no picnic table was available we took our folding table and chairs from the trailer. That saved us from eating on the ground, a procedure which is likely to take some of the joy from outdoor eating, especially for old folk with creaky joints. Also it protected us from ants. As someone has remarked, if ants are as industrious as they are reputed to be, how come they have time to attend all the picnics?

We picnicked beside famous Smith River in northern California, and beside even more famous Rogue River in Oregon. Beside rushing streams and beside placid lakes. In country parks, state parks, and national parks. Some of our most favored picnic spots were in U.S. Forestry camps, with which the forested areas of our country are richly endowed. Whenever no park or regular camp was at hand we pulled to the side of the road, turned our backs on the highway (the trailer door is on the right side and therefore well adapted for this), and as we ate looked off across the fields to the mountains. One great brown mountain, I recall, was crested with snow. Shirley said, "It looks like a chocolate sundae with marshmallow topping" — which shows where her mind was dwelling.

One of our pleasantest picnics was in the early evening. Oregon, in its extensive road-improvement program, has taken advantage of strips of abandoned pavement to create roadside turnoffs and picnic areas, thereby endearing the state to the traveling public.

About four o'clock one afternoon we came upon a particularly sightly one of these spots and stopped. It was on the bank of the Columbia River, at a place where that mighty stream is especially beautiful. In contrast to certain stretches where it is a roaring cataract, here it is wide and placid with small green islands dotting it. Since the afternoon was still warm, we got out our folding chairs and rested for a while in the shade of an overhanging tree. We enjoyed it so much that we decided to spend the night. As the sun got low, and the color reflections on the still water became most entrancing, we got out our folding table and ate our supper. It's strange the way little unimportant occurrences cling to your memory. I remember that as we sat there, enjoying the lovely sunset and its glorious reflections on the river, a truck driver rolling along the highway below us caught a glimpse of us out of the corner of his eye. His head jerked around and up for a better look. Then he smiled and waved a friendly greeting. We waved back.

Shirley said, "Bet he's saying to himself, 'Some people have all the luck!'" If so, he was exactly right. We felt that we were having all the good luck any two persons were entitled to.

We stayed here overnight. Which leads me to comment, picnics are not the only nice things about trailer travel. I remember back in the old vaudeville days seeing a skit that was supposedly laid in the front yard of a transplanted Englishman. He and his American next-door neighbor were having an altercation. Finally, in exasperation the Englishman said, "An Englishman's home is his castle." "Well then," the American replied, "you'd better go into your castle and pull up the drawbridge."

That suggests the way Shirley and I feel when night comes and we go into our little home-away-from-home and close the door. The world is shut outside and we are in our little castle, with the drawbridge up.

You develop a deep attachment for this Tom Thumb's Castle that goes with you through California and Oregon and Washington; through Maine and Georgia and Alabama; through Banff and Quebec and Nova Scotia; through Guadalajara and Mexico City and Acapulco. And so on and on, day after day and mile after mile. And at night, no matter where you are, gives you your own comfortable bed to rest in; and the next morning is ready to start on again, whatever direction your wandering spirit wishes to take. This is truly being at home on the open road.

During the evening, there on the bank of the Columbia, another trailer pulled in behind us. It was large for traveling: about thirty or thirty-five feet long, which made it roughly twice as big as ours. As soon as it stopped, a young couple got out, the woman carrying a baby in her arms. In friendly fashion they came over to get acquainted. After an exchange of greetings and some discussion of the weather, the roads, and the scenery, I remarked:

"Pretty good-size outfit you're hauling. Going far?"

"Alaska," calmly replied the man — who had made himself known as Randy Childs.

"Alaska!" Shirley and I exclaimed in unison.

"We're moving," the wife explained. "Randy has just graduated from Engineering College and is going to work on the Alcan Highway."

We expressed our concern over their attempt to pull so large a trailer so far.

"Others have made it, so can we," said Randy. "I've studied up on the highway. Don't expect any trouble."

"We want a good-size trailer when we get there," broke in the wife, "'cause we're going to live in it, least (she spoke with excited eagerness, clipping her words) till we know we like it and are going to stay."

Before we parted the next morning we asked them to write us a report on their trip when they got located in Alaska. That fall we heard from them announcing their safe arrival, and their satisfaction with the job and their trailer home and Alaska in general.

In Northeastern Washington we reached one of our objectives, the farm home of former Los Angeles neighbors, the Jorgensens. We parked our trailer beside the stream that runs through their farm, and stayed a few days. I'll have more to say about that visit later. It turned out to be one of those Y's in the road of human destiny.

After leaving the Jorgensens we went up into Canada. We followed the Kootenay River to Arrow Lakes, on to Kootenay Lake which we crossed by ferry, and on to the pleasant town of Cranbrook. There we found so charming a park to stay in that we stopped over for a few days. The park had broad shaded lawns green with grass and lawn clover. A clear cold stream flowed through the park. A sand-bordered pool was inviting to the town's children. And for adults there was about the biggest swimming pool we had ever seen. It had a husky young male lifeguard, and a beautifully constructed young female lifeguard. Colored lights reflected from the pool at night. And music records, soft and sweet, played all the time.

About one-third of this city park was roped off for trailers and campers. The trailer section was under tall pine trees. Next to us was one of those interesting characters you run into in trailer parks—to my mind the most interesting people in the world. This fellow was a horse doctor from, of all places, the Pribilof Islands. Traveling alone, he was deeply engrossed in his three hobbies, which were: dry fly fishing, golf (there was a nine-hole course near the trailer park), and catching bugs in nets. "When I don't have anything else to do," he told us, "I catch bugs." And proudly he showed us some of his impaled insects, calling attention to the intricate pattern of their wings as revealed through his magnifying glass. "Couldn't stay tied to my job any longer," he said. "Had to cut loose and give more time to my hobbies."

While in Cranbrook we took a run out to a lake that had been recommended for fishing, naturally taking the trailer along. We liked it so well we stayed a couple of days. It appeared at first that there was no one else within a hundred miles. But the next morning we realized that this had been a mistaken judgment, for a herd of cows came moseying along the edge of the woods near the lake. They were the only sign of civilization anywhere about. I remember the incident particularly because of a mad bull. He wasn't mad at us, indeed he paid no attention to us. He was mad at his harem. He came along an hour or so behind the cows, obviously giving them old Billy Hell for walking out on him. He wasn't hurrying to catch up. He'd strut along a few paces, then stop and paw the dirt, then move along a bit and stop and paw some more, all the time grumbling and cussing and making the most awful threats about what he was going to do to the girls when he caught up to them.

Another of our destinations was reached a few days later, Glacier National Park in Montana. In our book this park is unexcelled for beauty anywhere. We parked our trailer on the bank of tumbling Avalanche Creek. Our first picnic lunch here was followed by two surprises, one for Shirley and one for me. After we'd eaten I took a walk through the park, leaving Shirley relaxing over a cup of coffee. My surprise came in encountering, camped near us, a couple of trailer friends from Palm Springs, Ross and Mary Fraser, retired school people from Los Angeles. Meeting good friends in far places is exciting. I took them over to see Shirley. There we found that she had had a bit of excitement of her own.

While she was still sipping coffee, a bear cub came along and insisted on joining her. To discourage him, Shirley picked up a stone and threw it at him. Her aim must have been better than usual for she hit her mark. The cub took to a tree. Neighboring picnickers came to watch. They took pictures and made excited clamor. The now frightened little fellow climbed higher and higher. At last he reached the topmost branches, and stayed there. Considerable speculation was expressed by the onlookers as to what the mother bear would do when she came looking for her baby. But no one made a move to leave. Instead, more people continued to arrive. The mother bear did not come, and the cub clung to his high perch all afternoon — making Shirley ashamed of being such a good marksman. The cub was still in the treetop when we went to bed. But sometime during the night he disappeared.

Our third and most distant objective was Banff National Park. The high point here was meeting, by previous arrangement, two young friends from home.

Few satisfactions come to an old professor equal to his associations with up-and-coming young people. Such a satisfaction Shirley and I have found with the young couple who met us in Banff. We'll call them the Bertrands — not their real name. Carl, a former student of mine at UCLA had got his doctorate at another university and had then been brought back to UCLA to teach. Shortly a bond of friendship between them and us developed, a friendship which was intensified when it became known that we all four were fond of trailering. This summer while Shirley and I had been taking our leisurely trip north, Carl Bertrand had been teaching in summer school. Then, with the session over, Carl and his vivacious young wife Suzzanne made record time getting to Banff to meet us.

They did take time out along the way, however, for one side excursion. They regaled us with the account of it when we met. They stopped overnight at an Oregon coast resort famous for its razorback clams. In preparation for the clam-digging the next morning, they rented a "clam gun" — which they found to be nothing more than a narrow, long-bladed shovel.

"How do you find the clams?" they inquired of the man who rented them the "gun."

"Just look for a dimple in the sand," said he. "You'll see it right away after the wave goes out. Gotta dig fast," he warned, "them buggers can disappear like nobody's business."

The next morning bright and early they were on the beach. Almost at once Suzzanne spied a "dimple."

"Here's one," she said excitedly.

Carl set to work digging. But he uncovered no clam.

"Here's another," Suzzanne sang out. "Better dig faster."

Carl dug faster. And with each dimple that Suzzanne discovered, he dug faster and yet faster. The sweat poured off him. But he uncovered no clams.

The dimples, they noticed, made a row along the beach. They followed the row, Carl giving his all to the digging. But not a clam did he dig up.

Finally they came to a man sitting off to one side on the dry sand. As Carl and Suzzanne approached he arose and stood waiting for them, leaning on his cane.

"I've been watching you," he chuckled. "You've been digging up my cane tracks."

Together we and the Bertrands saw the sights: Banff, Lake Louise, Jasper Park, and numerous other beauty spots thereabouts. We swam in the naturally heated pools where you can choose the temperature you wish: 88 degrees, 96 degrees, 104 degrees. Nature caters to your individual taste.

Together we experimented with what appeared to be Alberta's favorite alcoholic beverage, equal parts of beer and tomato juice. By Alberta law patrons may finish the drinks before them when closing time arrives. So just before closing time the patrons stock up. It was quite a sight, the tables all loaded with alternate glasses of beer and tomato juice. Upon sampling the mixture, we decided it would not lure us into a lost weekend.

Together we picnicked. After one picnic at a bend of Bow River where we stopped on our way to Jasper Park, Suzzanne retired to their trailer for a little rest, Shirley went to our trailer to knit, and Carl and I took a walk along Bow River.

Returning from the walk some time later, Carl and I were startled by a piercing scream. Suzzanne's trailer door flew open and out she popped, still screaming. We rushed toward her.

"What's the trouble?" Carl shouted.

"Somebody peeked in my window," she called back. "Just a minute ago."

"Why," puffed Carl as we drew up to her, "there's nobody around here. Nobody within miles. You must've had a nightmare."

"Nightmare, my foot!" Suzzanne pointed to the trailer's rear window. "I tell you somebody was right there. Had a big shaggy head like a wild man's. Had little eyes like a pig's . . . Must have crawled up on his hands and knees, for all of a sudden he stood up and leaned on the window. Stared right in at me."

Just then Carl started to laugh. "There's your culprit," he said, pointing.

Startled by Suzzanne's screams the window-peeker — a black bear — had dropped back to his four feet and sneaked off through the trees. Now, in an opening, he paused to see what all the fuss was about. No doubt he had been looking for a handout and was not at all interested in Suzzanne's physical charms.

One day I persuaded Carl to go fishing with me the next morning. Carl was not an avid fisherman, especially when I told him how early I wanted to start.

"What's the matter?" he wanted to know. "Do you have to sneak up on them in the dark?"

But to an old fisherman, early morning and fishing have as natural an affinity as ham and eggs. I insisted on starting at daylight.

"All right then," said Suzzanne resignedly, "I'll get up and get breakfast for these night crawlers, Shirley. You stay in bed."

But Shirley got up, and the four of us had pancakes, Canadian bacon, and coffee in the Bertrands' trailer. Then Carl and I drove to the Vermillion Lakes.

We caught some trout that morning. But Carl was unhappy over his lack of skill with a fly rod and asked me to give him a bit of instruction in the art. While I was engaged in the instruction, up the road came a Royal Mountie. He parked his trusty steed, a motorcycle, and strode purposefully toward us. What a guilty feeling you get when a police officer strides purposefully toward you! Now what? I thought. I wondered if it was illegal to cast a fly line close to a public thoroughfare. That was the only thing I could think of. It didn't seem like a very serious offense. Still I felt guilty.

"How's it going?" he inquired.

"Pretty fair," we admitted. Then we waited impatiently for him to get on with the business at hand.

"Here, let me see that rod," he said. "I've had quite a lot of experience at this sort of thing. First you have to learn to hold the rod right. Like this . . ."

Then Carl and I both got a lesson in fly casting from an expert. And thereby this Mountie *got* his men. Both of us. To this day I have a kindlier feeling toward policemen.

Carl and I went back to the trailers and we four had another picnic, with trout.

Thus the summer went. Shirley and I look back upon the trip as our four-thousand-mile picnic.

When we got home to our stationary home, after the long vacation traveling in our home-away-from-home, the living room in our stationary home looked simply vast. Shirley joked about it.

"Why don't we just start a trailer park right here?" she said.

Just for fun I figured up the footage. And do you know, if we could have got them in through the wall we'd have had room for *four* trailers the size of our travel trailer right there in our living room.

It doesn't require a very big trailer to provide a comfortable home on the open road.

CHAPTER IV

SEARCHING FOR SHANGRI-LA

Nearly everyone dreams of some place where he hopes sometime to dwell, a spot which will be his individual end-of-the-rainbow.

Recently a popular writer asked ten celebrities, "Where is your own personal Shangri-La?" The ten notables, including such diverse personalities as Supreme Court Justice William O. Douglas, singers Rise Stevens and Frank Sinatra, actor Jackie Gleason, and golfer Sammy Snead, expressed dreams as diverse as their occupations. Varied as the dreams were, however, one element they had pretty much in common.

Of the entire group only one longed for a luxurious apartment or penthouse. All of the rest envisioned some quiet, relaxed place, close to nature and "far from the madding crowd."

I propose to tell you how two of us, strictly non-celebrities, namely my wife Shirley and I, found our dream spot. I'm going to let you in on the secret of how much it cost. And I'm going to give a little advice, based on our experience, on a good way for some of you to set about hunting for your own Shangri-Las.

It was during our stay with the Jorgensens—reported in Chapter III—that we found the forest retreat which has become our end-of-the-rainbow—that is, for summers.

Andy and Olga Jorgensen were eager to slough off the city's traffic, city noises, city nervous tensions, and — of considerable importance — city living costs. They wanted to get away to the type of country from which they had both come, farm country. After a long search they settled upon a retirement ranch among what they described as "tree-clad hills and lush cultivated valleys" north of Spokane, Washington. Their farm, they exulted, was 75 miles from the nearest city. They urged us to come and see their find.

From our first sight of their country place we considered the district to be as beautiful as they pictured it. We parked our trailer on the bank of the Jorgensens' stream and set up housekeeping. At their insistence we made free use of the vegetables in their garden: fresh peas, beans, carrots, young beets, tomatoes, and green corn. At *our* insistence, we paid for fresh eggs, milk and cream, and dressed chickens and ducks.

We had been there only a few days when tall, slow-speaking Andy said, "I shouldn't be surprised if the place next to us could be bought pretty reasonably."

"Uh-uh," I said real fast. In contrast to the Jorgensens with their farm background, I scarcely knew one end of a plow from the other, and neither did Shirley. Neither of us had any urge to begin, at our years, an intimate acquaintanceship with farm labor. "No farm for us, thank you."

"It isn't a farm," Andy assured us. "It's a strip of land that was cut off from a big farm when the county put the new hard-surface road through." Then he added with his slow emphasis. "But it's something special. Better take a look at it."

We took the look — and were lost. We knew that if the plot could be bought, and within our budget, we wanted it.

"What makes you think the owner would be willing to sell?" I asked.

"Can't get his cows onto it," replied Andy. "Tried to drive them through the culvert, but they wouldn't drive. So it's no good to him for pasturage. And he has plenty of other wood plots and springs. He doesn't need this."

The owner proved to be a friendly farmer with blarney on his tongue. "Why, yes," he replied in response to our inquiry, "we might consider selling it . . . to the right people. Wouldn't you say so, Ma?"

Ma agreed. But when it came to settling on a price, he hesitated. I didn't have much of an idea how much he might ask. I knew that the district is too far off the beaten path to have enjoyed — or suffered, whichever way you look at it — a land boom. But I was pleasantly surprised when he finally said, "Hate to ask it . . . seems like a lot of money for undeveloped land. But because of those blue spruces and the spring and the stream, we'll have to ask you a hundred dollars an acre."

I agreed to the price real quick before he had a chance to change his mind. The plot, extending about one thousand feet along the paved road, is roughly 400 feet wide at one end and comes to a point at the other end. Mr. Long estimated that it contained about three acres. And that was close enough for us. Three acres: $300.

The attitude of hating to charge we have found to be typical of the neighborhood. During the years since we bought the plot we have had occasion to call upon several of our farm neighbors for help of one kind or another: bulldozing a road through our trees, hauling fire bricks from town for an outdoor fireplace I built, helping me tile in the spring and build a cover over it, digging a cesspool, and other services of like nature. Invariably the charge, if any, is made with reluctance and apology. I hadn't known that such people still existed in the world.

We call our plot Springbrook Woods, a fancy name — but then, we think it's a pretty fancy place. Only three acres, but what a three acres! The spring is a bubbling well of pure, sweet-tasting water. The brook although small — in some places I can jump across it, and

I can't jump half as far as I could forty or fifty years ago — sings a sweet song that lulls us to sleep nights and is a constant source of delight daytimes. The trees are pines, firs, larches (locally called tamaracks), and — the pride of the place — handsome blue spruces, as shapely and decorative as any trees that grow in the forest.

Our first improvement was a most important structure — since the 16-foot trailer we owned at that time did not have a bathroom. We selected a spot hidden in a cluster of spruce trees. Using the services of a neighbor who is skilled with hammer and saw (at $1.50 an hour), we erected our w.c. Last summer when electricity was brought to our "ranch," making available the sanitary facilities in our present modern travel trailer, we converted this structure into a storage house.

In addition to other charms, our area has game. One day last summer Shirley and I were on our way to the village nine miles away where we do our shopping, when a family of half-grown pheasants crossed the road in front of us. I jammed on the brakes as quickly as I could, and the birds scurried as fast as *they* could, but one laggard didn't quite make it. We thought at first that we had hit him, then we thought we hadn't, for when we glanced back we saw no dead or fluttering bird. We went on to town, parked on the main street, did our errands, and got nearly home, still thinking ourselves innocent. But upon stopping at a neighbor's for a chat, the little girl walked past the front of our car, looked surprised, and said, "What have you got this bird on the front of your car for?" Upon investigation I found the pheasant caught back of and nearly hidden by our license plate. I do not know what the law is dealing with such cases. All I know is, the bird made a delectable meal.

There are many deer. One neighbor had the front of his car bashed in by one that tried to jump over his hood. Another neighbor's children have a pet fawn that has become as tame as a lamb. One evening shortly before dusk when Shirley and I were driving to a neighbor's for red raspberries — at twenty cents a quart — we counted over a dozen deer that had come out of the woods and were feeding in hay fields.

Once on a fishing trip with the postmaster of a nearby village, driving along a country road through thick woods, we rounded a curve and came suddenly upon a bear cub in the road. He had a shiny black coat with a white blaze on his chest, and was cute as a roly-poly puppy. Being unarmed we spent no time hunting for mama bear, who doubtless was somewhere in the vicinity. Seeing us the cub scurried off the road into the woods and disappeared.

Along our stream I have encountered ducks, grouse (locally called native pheasants), and wild mink. Once a little brown weasel lay in a pile of brush and stared up at me defiantly, seeming to have his fierce eyes fixed on my jugular vein and estimating its availability.

I left him strictly alone. So I did with a handsome black-and-white skunk that came, waving his tail like a flaunting banner, down to our stream to drink. I took the attitude "live and let live," and he did the same for me.

My rarest experience was with a beaver. In a thick clump of alder trees on a neighbor's farm is a large beaver pond. Fishing near it one day, I stole up to the dam. I was lucky. A beaver was working at the other end of the dam, the first I ever saw at work in his native haunts. He was doing a repair job. He would swim to the head of the pond and bring back a mouthful of twigs, which he would tuck into a weak spot in the dam. After each such trip he would dive to the bottom and come up with a gob of mud atop his nose. He would push the mud around the twigs to seal them into place. Gradually, he worked in my direction, examining every foot of the dam as he came. So absorbed was he in his job that for some time he did not notice me. When only a few feet away he sensed that something was not as it should be. He peered in my direction, but since I stood motionless he could not be sure of what was wrong. He lay still, his broad tail stretched out on top of the water, his eyes fixed steadily in my direction. Cautiously he moved closer, his nose twitching. Suddenly a wayward breeze must have carried him my scent, for suddenly he slapped his tail on the water making a sound like the crack of a rifle; and he was gone, leaving only a swirl of water where he had been.

In the evening, that hushed time of day that Olga Jorgensen calls the enchanted hour, we sit outside our trailer and watch the peaceful night come on. For a long time we were mystified by an odd sound in the quiet sky; it was like the zooming of a miniature plane making a power dive. But once, idly watching the night hawks that were circling above us, I saw one of them climb high into the heavens and then make a "power dive" straight down. Shortly after came the zoom. The mystery was solved.

Another phase of nature that we enjoy is the wildflowers. From the wild forget-me-not plants that grow at the stream's edge and nod and dip their tiny blue flowers into the stream's ripples, to the tall wild syringas that grow along the fences and fill the air with the fragrance of the waxy flowers, we seem never to be without blossoms. Violets, bluebells, wild snapdragons, shooting stars, fireweed, and a host of other flowers distribute themselves throughout the season. Nature appears deliberately to hold back some varieties until others have had their turn, so that there always may be color and beauty.

The words of a poet come to mind: "What is this life if, full of care, we have no time to stand and stare?" Well, in our forest retreat we take time to stand and stare. And so, we were happy to learn, do many of our farmer neighbors. One of these, a bachelor whom we'll call Hank, has the soul of a nature poet, but lacks some of the poet's power of expression. His oft-repeated observation is "No sir, you can't beat nature." But Hank gives a practical slant to his love of nature. While others around him are selling their timber for high prices, Neighbor Hank refuses to sell. His pines and firs tower over the surrounding country, making timber buyers drool when they drive by. Hank lights his house with kerosene lamps. He drives a car that is old enough to vote. He lacks many of today's comforts and conveniences. But he *won't* sell his timber. One day, standing with him and admiring his great trees, I pointed to a giant pine. "Hank," I said, "what would that tree bring on the market?"

He stood for a minute with his stubble-covered face lifted so he could gaze to the top of the great tree. "I reckon that tree might fetch as much as seventy-five dollars," he said. Then he added hastily, "But it ain't going to. That pine brings more than seventy-five dollars worth of satisfaction to me, and to other folks too. No sir, them trees will be standing right where they are till after I'm gone."

We like our neighbors.

But I shouldn't make it appear that there are no snakes in our Garden of Eden. Actually there are none of the poisonous varieties, but we do have an occasional garter snake to make Shirley jump and emit a ladylike squeal. We sometimes have wasps that gather when we start to cook outdoors. They like the smell of cooking meat; and by the way they hover round us we imagine they consider meat "on the hoof" as rather tasty too; but they haven't yet attacked us with either end. Sometimes our neighbors' cows break through our fence and pay us uninvited visits. One day we saw a stray cow on the highway in front of our place. Thinking it had broken out of Walter Long's woods pasture, as his cows sometimes do, Shirley and I undertook to drive it back in. Figuring that even a cow, stupid as they are, should know how to get back in where it came out, one of us got in front of it and the other behind and we drove it back and forth along the fence. But the ornery critter couldn't or wouldn't find the place. After long, fruitless, and sweat-producing labor, we gave up. But in order to get it off the highway we drove it through our open gate into our wood plot. I hopped into our car and drove up to Long's. There I found overall-clad Walter Long just unhitching his work team.

"One of your cows got out of the pasture again," I told him. "We've got it down at our place."

"Thought I had that fence fixed," said Walter. "I'll be dogged."

He rode back with me. On the way I told him of our unsuccessful attempts to drive the cow back through the fence into his pasture. When we got there, Walter first examined the fence, then looked quizzically at me.

"Can't see where she got through," he said. "Let's have a look at her."

He took one look at the cow, placidly grazing on our clover lawn, and shook his head. "No wonder . . ." He seemed to be having trouble keeping his face straight. "No wonder you had yourselves a time trying to drive her through our fence. That ain't our cow."

But the next day he brought us a dressed chicken for our good intentions.

One June day, a couple of years ago, as we arrived at our woodland plot after the trip from California, we drove along the woods road through the overhanging trees, reveling in the greenness everywhere and the fresh woodsy smell. Then as we reached the clearing where we set up our trailer, Shirley exclaimed, "Living in clover!" She was referring to our ground clover. We planted the lawn clover seed when we bought the place and the seed has responded so nobly that now we have a carpet of velvety green, patterned and perfumed with white clover blossoms. But Shirley also had in mind the slang use of the phrase, for up there we do feel that we're "living in clover."

It was around four o'clock in the afternoon. Our little stream looked so inviting that I suggested, "Mind if I put off till morning setting up the trailer?" By "setting up," I meant connecting the electricity, water, and sanitary facilities, and leveling the trailer on its semi-permanent blocks. The blocks are used when we stay in one spot for several days, giving a feeling of solidness to the trailer. On shorter stops we don't use them.

"No," said Shirley. "I'll settle for just the electricity."

I hurriedly hooked up the electricity and got my trout rod from its storage tube under the trailer. The trout in our stream, like the stream itself, are not large: six, seven, eight inches, with occasionally an old lunker of ten, eleven, or even (rarely) twelve inches. They are native rainbows. In less than two hours I was back with enough of the delectable fellows for our supper and our breakfast.

Such is our summer Shangri-La. For this woodland paradise we have spent, with original investment and improvements — including a good used electric pump which brings running water from the spring into our trailer and, our latest addition, a good-sized cabaña— about $800.

"But," you may protest, "look at how far you have to drive to get there."

It's true. We do have quite a trip every time we go to our little end-of-the-rainbow. The shortest route from our winter home in the desert near Palm Springs to this northern summer place is close to fifteen hundred miles. And we don't always take the shortest route, which is through Reno, Nevada, and nearly straight north from there. Sometimes we go through California's redwood forests, travel along Oregon's dramatic coastline, and skirt Washington's fabulous bays, before we strike off across the Cascades to our retreat. And sometimes we come home by Idaho's Lake Coeur d'Alene and Salmon River, Utah's fruit orchards, and Nevada's glamorous gambling resort, Las

Vegas. Part of the joy of our Shangri-La is the pleasure of the trip by trailer.

I haven't pinpointed the exact location of our dream spot. Our tiny trout stream couldn't withstand the onslaught of a horde of city slickers with trout rods. Besides, part of the pleasure you will find in *your* El Dorado will come from locating it for yourself.

Where will you find your Shangri-La?

Tastes differ so, and sections of our country differ so, it's hard to answer that question. Of one thing you may be pretty sure, you won't find your relaxed, quiet, unexploited country place in the shadow of any courthouse. You may have to look far, especially if land prices have any weight in your planning. Therefore, I suggest that you get a trailer to help in your search.

I pause right here to aver that I have no financial interest, in any shape, form, or manner, in the trailer industry. This advice comes purely under the head of "remarks for the good of the order."

Yes, you may have to take a lot of time and do a lot of driving before you find that dream spot. And even then, without doubt, there is a bit of luck involved. But this I can say, and do say — provided you are anything like Shirley and me — if you get a nice little travel trailer and start hunting, even though you fail to find the absolutely perfect dream spot, you are going to have a lot of fun looking.

CHAPTER V

HIGH ADVENTURE ON A LOW BUDGET

The guide, a heavy-set man of medium height, sat facing me in the end of the boat. He shifted his weight and looked me squarely in the eyes, his level gaze questioning.

"Like to try it in The Row?" he said.

By "The Row" I knew he was referring in guarded language to the string of boats out toward the mouth of the river. Usually it was called "Anchor Row," or, lugubriously, "Suicide Row."

This was back some ten years ago, before the enactment of certain safety regulations which now govern fishing on the river. At that time reports of drownings were not uncommon. The term "Suicide Row," although used whimsically, was not altogether inappropriate.

For several hours we had been trolling in the relatively placid "bay" where the river broadened widely before narrowing to rush through a slender channel into the ocean. Fishing had been unproductive both for us and for the dozens upon dozens of other boats that competed with us for space. The whole bay was pack-jammed, like a dance floor too full of couples for anything but the slowest, most careful maneuvering. That was how we had been trolling, slowly and carefully, trying to avoid collisions. But despite our care, repeatedly we had been bumped. Sometimes we bantered with the occupants of the other boats. But at other times, when our lines crossed and tangled, we exchanged looks, and under-our-breath words, that were far from banter! I was ready for a change. But The Row . . . ? I hesitated.

"Don't want to influence you," said the guide, "but I fig'er with a good boat and," he added significantly, "a good guide, you're 'bout as safe there as most any place on the river. Whole lot safer than on the streets of . . . where'd you say you come from?"

"Los Angeles."

"Yeah, Los Angeles. Ain't nobody safe on them streets."

Already I had begun to wonder if my extravagence in hiring a guide — that was how I looked at it, an extravagence — was going to be a complete fizzle. I hadn't even had a strike. But from long experience I knew how quickly a man's luck could change, and I hadn't completely given up hope of getting at least a little action for my money. Maybe, I thought, the guide's suggestion is the answer. At any rate, nothing ventured . . . I nodded.

The guide advanced his accelerator and the motor responded

with a smooth, competent roar. As we moved swiftly toward the string of boats, I could sense the guide's eyes covertly looking me over, sizing me up, no doubt wondering what I would do in an emergency, of which there was always a possibility. I was sure he'd spotted me for a greenhorn at salmon fishing, which I was. Trout fishing in mountain lakes and streams, preferably streams, had always been my kind of fishing. Salmon fishing was a new experience. That was why I'd hired a guide.

Swiftly we bore down on the string of boats. Each was tied to the one next to it, making a row that extended about halfway across the river. Although much closer to the river's mouth than were the bay trollers, still these boats seemed to be a safe distance — several hundred feet — back from the place where the broad, smooth-surfaced river narrowed to a funnel between towering rocks and went swirling and churning toward the ocean breakers just beyond. The heavy booming of the breakers came plainly, and a little disturbingly, to my ears. Here, however, the river appeared safe enough, a broad smooth sheet of moving water.

These Row fishermen, I concluded, were as close to the river's vortex as their courage, or possibly the Coast Guard's regulations, would permit. Their purpose, naturally, was to get first crack at the salmon as they breasted the river's current, following their instinct to spawn somewhere upriver.

When within forty or fifty feet of the boats, the guide slowed his motor and motioned for me to drop the anchor.

"Play the rope out real slow," he cautioned. "I'll keep the motor going till we get tied to the others . . . Slow and easy now. Ee-a-sy . . . We'll let the rope out a good piece. That'll give the anchor more bite."

He watched me for a minute to see that I was following instructions, then turned back to fit us into our place at the end of the line. I saw his start of surprise. For the first time he noticed, and I noticed, a gap of open water between the last boat in the row and a single boat anchored just beyond. The guide hesitated, then quickly reached a decision. Instead of seeking the comparative safety of a tie-up with The Row, he was swinging our boat over next to the "maverick." Quite obviously he had decided that the boat's occupants might need help, and some innate sense of chivalry had triumphed over his caution.

"Kind'a risky out here by yourselves, ain't it?" he asked the couple in the boat.

Up to that time I had not paid any particular attention to the occupants other than to note that they were elderly. Now, shocked, I observed that the woman was a cripple whom I had seen on the dock. Hobbling along on crutches, she had attracted my attention partly because she was a woman in a group composed predominantly of men, even more because she most certainly was the only woman on crutches. But there was something else that distinguished her. In the crowd of people buying tackle, renting boats, hiring guides, organizing fishing parties, pushing, jostling, she stood out mainly because of a certain . . . gaiety? . . . in her facial expression. It was a quality of manner and expression hard to define. It reminded me of a small child off on some great lark, bubbling over with excitement. As I watched I saw her stop, switch the crutches to one hand and use the free hand to wipe sweat beads from her face. The day was not hot. Obviously walking was painful business. But that look of child-like exuberance never left her face. I was glad to see that she could stand free from the crutches' support, was not entirely helpless without them. Still she had looked oddly out of place there on the dock. She looked even more out of place in this lone boat off the end of The Row.

Instead of answering the guide the man stood up, whirled his hook and sinker around his head, and heaved them far down the river.

The guide, looking startled, protested, "You don't have to do that. Just drop your bait in the water. Current'll carry it out far enough."

As before, the man paid no attention. A minute later, as if to show his defiance, he reeled in his line, stood up, took another healthy swing, and threw the bait even farther.

The guide turned to me, his face stern. "Don't *you* stand up. No matter if you get a fish on. No matter what happens, don't stand up under no circumstances. The river's current combined with the outgoing tide generates a lot of power. This water can be dangerous."

It seemed to me that he was being unnecessarily bossy. I could see that there was potential danger all right. The seething cauldron swirling through the funnel out toward the ocean showed that. So did the regular booms of the breakers beyond. But that was quite a way off. Right here the water flowed smoothly. There were none of the swirling eddies and white foam one associates with treacherous rapids.

Sensing my attitude, the guide said, "Look here, let me show you something."

He reached under his seat and brought out a folded newspaper. I smiled inwardly, thinking: This guy is a bit of a showoff. That newspaper didn't just *happen* there. He's prepared for this. Probably done whatever it is he's going to do many times before, to impress other greenhorns. There was a dramatic flourish in the very way he plunged the paper over the boat's side and held it submerged. The showman's technique, I thought. The big ham!

But before the demonstration was over, my whole estimate of the procedure changed. I concluded he was justified in using all the dramatic skill he possessed to drive home the lesson. When the paper was thoroughly soaked and he released it, it darted off, still submerged, with the speed of a swooping hawk.

I glanced over to see how the couple were taking the demonstration. They weren't even looking. The man was busy reeling in, preparatory to another cast, which he again stood up to deliver. The woman was watching him. On her face was that same expression of happy excitement that had never left her. They were, I decided, a strange pair.

But pretty soon the woman gave us a clue; she couldn't hold back any longer.

"Isn't this wonderful? Salmon fishing! Never thought *I'd* have anything like this." She shook her head in wonderment, again reminding me of a small child incredulous at her unexpected good fortune. She didn't actually look down at her crippled legs, but you could tell she was thinking of them. "Look at this!" she exulted. Stooping over she lifted a large, silver-sided fish from the bottom of the boat. "*Two* of them!" she exclaimed.

That perhaps was explanation enough for her gaiety. But still she hadn't given us the answer to the big question: How did she come to be there? She left that for us to speculate upon. And I speculated. Was this, I wondered, a late-in-life honeymoon? Could be.

I turned my attention to the man. He was about as hard to fathom as she was. Under medium height, narrow sloping shoulders, pale; he was, I decided, a bit on the puny side. Idly meditating, I built up a mental picture of his background. A lonely old bachelor, passed by in the race for success. A recluse, soured on life. Then had come an acquaintanceship with an understanding woman; a woman who through her own suffering had developed an unusual supply of empathy. For the first time in his lonely life he had found someone who cared. Then, finally, the crowning achievement of his life, a woman's love. He was in spirit a small boy reveling in his first girl's adoration. He was showing off.

That is where my idle speculation led me. It was a pleasant whimsey . . . My musings were interrupted by a sudden fierce jerk on my line. Galvanized into action, I gave the rod a quick, hard pull. The line came free. I reeled in to find my bait — a minnow the guide had fastened on the hook — stripped clean. There was nothing left but a head and bony skeleton.

"Take it easy," admonished the guide. "Not quite so fast next time. And don't jerk so hard."

For some time I sat tense and expectant, hoping for a return engagement with the fish. But after a while I relaxed and sat back. Since there was no further action on my line, or on anyone else's in the vicinity, I returned to my daydreaming. Only this time my mind went back to that matter of my extravagance — my Scotch instincts at work.

On our way down the coast from Washington, Shirley and I had got to talking about expenses, trailering, and my prospective retirement which loomed just a little ahead. Living as cheaply as we did summers in our Washington retreat, and even when traveling back and forth between California and Washington, paying only from $1 to $2 a night instead of the $5 to $10 a motel might charge, to say nothing of the savings effected by cooking our own meals in the trailer — well, we decided we were getting along all right; the future, even on a restricted retirement income, no longer looked frightening. So, as we touched at one after another of the coast towns, and saw the catches of salmon being brought in at night, I began to get that terrific fisherman's . . . urge. And as . . . we got closer and closer to the famous salmon river that I had been reading about for years, and I got more and more fidgety, Shirley took pity on me and said, "Why don't you stop over a day or two and do some salmon fishing? Only . . . " she added hesitantly, "I'd feel safer if you hired a guide." I wasn't hard to persuade. I hired the guide. And here I was, my $20 shot and the day slipping away with no salmon.

I chanced to glance over at our neighbors. Catching my eye, the woman smiled. That same beaming effulgence. The overflowing of a heart made joyous by unexpected fulfillment . . . Anyhow, that's how I had figured it out. And I thought: My money wasted? Uh-uh! I was being privileged to witness what appeared to be a wonderful Indian Summer in two lonely lives. I was getting my money's worth.

Again came that fierce jerk, throwing a bomb into the midst of my musings. This time the jerk was harder, more solid, more exciting. With a pull of my rod I set the hook, and the fight was on. And what a fight!

I had on previous occasions caught some husky trout. As a boy in Michigan I had caught some big pike. Once in more recent years, on one of my rare ocean-fishing trips, I had caught a large sea bass. But never had I experienced anything like this. On the end of my line was something that felt like the irresistible force. Up to the surface the fish surged. Down to the depths it plummeted. My reel was singing. Once the fish made a run under the boat, bending my rod almost double over the boat's side. Impulsively, I started to rise.

"Sit still," said the guide, quietly but firmly. "Let him have more line."

I sat down and the fight went on. Run after run of seemingly uncheckable power, followed by slow, muscle-straining retrieves of line. Finally, after what seemed like an hour but may have been fifteen or twenty minutes, the fish began to tire. The rushes became less power-packed, the retrieves easier. And at last I was able to lead the great gleaming fish to the boat. The guide dipped the net and lifted it from the water. He hit the fish on the head with a sort of billy club that he referred to as "the priest, administering the last rites." He held the fish aloft.

"Chinook," he said, admiring its shining beauty. "Nice one. Should go close to twenty pounds."

It was as if this was what he'd been waiting for, for now he said, "Time to go in."

I glanced around. Preoccupied, I had failed to notice that several of the other boats had already pulled away. The Row had closed ranks with each departure, and now was considerably shortened. The guide started our motor, giving it time to warm up. When it was purring smoothly he motioned for me to lift the anchor. As I started to comply the woman for the first time showed some apprehension.

"Don't you think we should go in, too, Henry?" she said to the man. "I wish we could get started before they leave."

Henry exhibited a suggestion of a boy's condescension toward a girl's timidity. "All right, Lilly, if you're scared." He turned to us, "Mind holding up a minute till I get my motor started and the anchor in?" Then, as if to apologize for Lilly's timidity, he added, "Motor isn't working too good. Stopped on us once or twice while we were trolling this morning."

"Criminy, man!" the guide exclaimed, "you out here with a defective motor?"

Without response Henry pulled his motor rope and the motor started. He smiled triumphantly at the guide. Then pushing past Lilly he stepped to the front of the boat and pulled in the anchor. Meanwhile Lilly had been holding their boat to the side of ours. When Henry started back to his seat, thoughtlessly he brushed past Lilly on the side next to our boat. With unconscious courtesy she released her hold to let him pass. Quickly the boat started to drift away.

Then things happened fast.

Lilly grabbed to regain her hold, but handicapped by her crippled legs she could not shift her body quickly enough. The gap had become too wide.

Jumping from the prow of our boat where I had been perched ready to pull in the anchor, I stretched as far over the side of our boat as I dared. But the prow of their boat had swung out rapidly. The distance was too great. I had to make a quick adjustment of my weight to avoid tumbling into the water.

But, I thanked heaven, the stern of their boat was still fairly close to the stern of ours. Reaching out a strong hand the guide grasped the side of their boat near its stern. The prow of their boat continued to drift out but the rear part was pinioned in the guide's muscular grip. He worked the boat around so that the rear part of the boat's side rested against the stern of our boat, leaving the front of their boat sticking out at a 90° angle. The guide's body was twisted around in an awkward position, but he seemed to be holding their boat safely. I breathed a sigh of relief — a relief that was short-lived.

"Can't hold it long like this," the guide panted.

I flung myself onto my knees in front of him, reached around his broad back and grasped the boat's wet slippery side close to its rear corner. The boat was tugging as if pulled by a steam engine.

Meanwhile, when Henry realized what was happening he dived for the end of his boat, grasped the throttle and gave it a mighty jerk. Instead of accelerating, the motor sputtered and died. Now, almost directly over my head, he was working with frantic haste, winding and yanking his starter rope. To no avail. The flooded carburetor did not emit even a cough of response. But Henry kept on trying, frantically and futilely.

The guide raised his voice in a shout. "Help!" and then again, "HELP!"

One of the trollers, a lone occupant of a boat who had ventured closer to The Row than had the others, heard the shout, reeled in his line and raced toward us.

The guide spoke to me in a low voice, as if not wanting the other two to hear for fear they'd panic. "Reason I yelled, we're drifting. Our anchor won't hold both boats."

I glanced at The Row. We had left it some distance behind. I looked at the shore where hundreds of shore fishermen stood almost shoulder to shoulder. Slowly we were slipping past them. I looked ahead. The great rocks that funneled the river were noticeably closer.

Once near us, the would-be rescuer grew cautious. He slowed his motor and circled, keeping a respectful distance from the boat athwart our stern.

"Give us a hand," the guide called. "We need help."

"See what I can do," the man replied. But he continued his cautious reconnoitering. It took him a harrowing length of time to decide upon a course of action. And when he did start to act, I was far from convinced he was doing the right thing — even though at the moment I couldn't think of anything better. Warily he pulled alongside us, still keeping a good distance from the old couple's boat. Apparently he had decided that he couldn't handle the loose boat by himself, but figured that by linking his boat to ours, the two motors could handle the three boats. I was skeptical because I couldn't see how he was going to establish a connection with us; certainly, neither the guide nor I had a free hand to help. Gradually he edged closer, working the stern of his boat toward the prow of ours. Then tragedy struck. A slight shift in the current swung the end of his boat over our taut anchor rope — and severed it cleanly. Instantly our two boats were racing away from the would-be rescuer, and toward the vortex.

"Gotta let go," gasped the guide. But reluctant to do so, for another minute he hung doggedly on. Sensing what would happen when he did let go, I redoubled my efforts. My whole body tensed with the strain. I've got to hold on, I thought. I've *got* to. My hands cramped and my fingers ached. My teeth gritted until my jaws hurt. Every muscle of my body was trying to transmit its strength to my fingers. But when the guide groaned under his breath "I *gotta* let go," and released his grip, all my concentration and all my tensing were useless. The boat tore out of my fingers as if they had been made of butter. The old couple's boat shot off toward the funnel.

Sick with chagrin I sank back on my heels. I felt like throwing up. But I could not turn away from the awful spectacle. With that terrible nausea gripping at my stomach, I watched the boat rush on at an ever-accelerating speed. The crippled Lilly sat rigid and helpless. Henry, finally abandoning his futile efforts with the starter rope, dropped the rope and seized the oars. With a fury of struggle he tried to row upstream. But he might as well have tried to row up Niagara Falls. Faster and faster the boat raced, until in horror I saw it swoop into the funnel.

With the guide's hands free to operate our motor, it responded with a roar of power. For a second, though, the boat seemed to be held in the grip of the river. It seemed to tremble and to be undecided as to which way to go. Then slowly it began to pull ahead, and in another minute we were out of danger.

"Hadda do it," the guide groaned.

You don't need to justify yourself to me, I thought. I'm the guilty one. My hand was the last to grasp their boat. If only — I groaned aloud — if only I'd had more grip in my hands.

But still the guide wanted to talk. All day long he had been far from talkative, saying only what needed to be said. But now his taciturnity had all evaporated. He talked a steady stream, still striving to justify his actions.

"Couldn't do a thing for them. Not a thing. Sure hope the Coast Guard can save that woman Lilly. The pipsqueak don't matter much. But that Lilly! Ever see anybody so happy? Sure hope they can get her in. They've saved some, you know. Wonderful organization . . . "

And so he talked on. I knew he didn't really consider "the pipsqueak" to be expendable. He was just giving expression to his pique over Henry's stubbornness. We both knew that to at least one person Henry was a pretty important individual. With him lost, Lilly would look upon her own rescue as pointless.

As we approached a landing place on the narrow strip of land that separates the river from the ocean, I beheld a scene of great excitement. The milling throng — which consisted of the vast number of shore fishermen, dozens of trollers who had landed ahead of us, many Indian fishermen and guides from the Reservation through which the river flowed, scores of Indian children, and dogs unnumbered — seemed to be a confused mass, undirected and purposeless, except to watch the thrilling action out in the surf.

Beaching our boat, we hurried up a small eminence where we could see what was going on. There we had a ringside view of as tense a drama as I ever expect to see.

Both Lilly and Henry were in the water, but separated by a distance of several hundred feet. Henry, directly in front of us, was in the middle of the breakers. His head showed dark in the white surf. A wave would wash him in toward shore, and for a minute it would look as if he would be brought all the way in. Then a receding wave would catch him and carry him back out. I could not detect any movement in his arms or legs. Apparently he had spent all his energy and was now a helpless gob of flesh at the breakers' mercy.

But as we watched, order seemed to be coming to the mob. It readily became apparent that someone had taken charge. A human chain was being organized. A tall, strongly built man carrying a coil of rope, took his place at the head of the line. They moved toward the water. At their first step into the surf the guide turned and raced up the beach. I wanted to follow, for I had a consuming urge to learn what was happening to Lilly. But the drama here was too tense. I could not pull away.

Gingerly the human chain made its way through the surf, each man holding a firm grip on the waist of the man ahead, leaving the leader's arms free for action with the rope. As they slowly advanced they were alternately pushed back and then sucked ahead by the waves. Every step was a battle for footing. But slowly, surely, they forged ahead. When out where each incoming wave inundated their bodies above their waists, they stopped. To go farther would be suicide.

It was close enough. The leader cast his rope like a lariat. It fell close to Henry. I was gratified to see his arm come up, even though feebly. He failed to grasp it, and was washed out beyond the possibility of reach. But in another minute he was washed in again. And with the next cast he caught the rope and hung on. With the human chain inching its way back to shore, Henry in tow, I turned and ran after the guide. He had disappeared in the throng. But the action out in the ocean was too tense for me to spend time hunting for him. I concentrated on what was happening to Lilly.

Nearer the river's mouth than Henry had been by at least three or four hundred feet, Lilly was clinging to the boat. The boat was upright with Lilly in the water beside it, her arm clamped over its side. The boat was bobbing like a cork. For a minute I could not understand why they were not washed in toward shore, as Henry had been, instead of remaining practically stationary in relation to the shore, only bobbing up and down with each incoming and receding wave. Then I saw the boat's anchor rope leading down into the water and realized what had happened. The boat had partly capsized, spilling both Lilly and Henry, and the anchor too, into the ocean. Then it had righted itself, empty. The anchor had stuck on the ocean bottom. Henry had been washed away. Lilly had clamped an arm — an arm made powerful by years of swinging her body on crutches — over the side of the boat. There she had clung during Henry's rescue. And there she still clung — but for how long? How long could any human being withstand the buffeting she was getting? While the boat did not move vertically, horizontally the movement was fierce. Though the boat was out beyond the worst of the breakers — otherwise the anchor would not have held — the swells were enormous. The boat was first high, then low, and each descent was accompanied by a resounding crash. A man near me put my own thoughts into words, "Great God, how long can she *take* that?"

A woman nearby used similar words but hers were in a prayer, uttered aloud. "Oh, dear God, don't, *don't* let her drown, she's been so brave."

But now a new phase of the drama began to unfold. Out between "The Jaws," as the two huge rocks that funneled the river were called, riding the churning outgoing current, came a boat somewhat larger than a rowboat carrying five men whom I assumed must be the Coast Guard crew. Four of the men each manned a single oar. The fifth, a man of enormous breadth of shoulder, sat in the stern acting as coxswain, directing the cadence of the oars.

Out where the full force of the river dissipated itself into the ocean, well out beyond the breakers, the boat stopped. The oarsmen poised their oars above the water. They appeared to be watching, waiting. Then it came, an incoming swell larger than most. The men bent to their oars. With hurtling speed they surged ahead, bearing down upon Lilly.

When they got close to the spot where she clung to her plunging boat — resembling for all the world a killer-bronco with the thrown rider clinging for dear life to the saddle — at the precise minute, with perfect timing, the oarsmen leaned on their oars in a backstroke, thus slightly checking the boat's forward speed. The coxswain, with the same perfect timing, swung his powerful arms over the side and seized Lilly. Straightening, he dragged her into the boat. The oarsmen bent to their oars and the boat shot ahead.

Now what? I wondered. They can't come to shore through those breakers. They'll swamp sure.

And they didn't try. They rode the rollers at an angle, headed in the general direction of the river, and moving only indirectly toward shore.

"They'll never make that either." I must have spoken aloud, for a man near me answered.

"Oh, yes, they will. They'll make it all right now. The worst is over. I've seen them do this before. Watch!"

And as I watched I began to understand their strategy. Adroitly they were maneuvering the boat into the exact spot where the edge of the outgoing river and the incoming breakers partially neutralized each other. It was a place of whirling eddies, but at that it was much calmer water than in the breakers elsewhere. With the perfectly coordinated strength of the four well-trained oarsmen, the boat was literally hurled through the eddies.

Touching shore, the four oarsmen jumped out and quickly hauled the boat up on the beach to safety. The coxswain lifted Lilly and carried her ashore.

Later that night, lying in my bed, I couldn't sleep. Usually I sleep better in the trailer than at home. But not that night. Every time I'd close my eyes my mind would skip away to the drama on the beach. I'd see Lilly, after the rescue, deprived of her crutches which no doubt were floating somewhere in the Pacific, leaning heavily on the coxswain. While waiting for the return of a man who had volunteered to bring his Jeep and transport the rescued couple to town, Lilly refused to lie or even sit on the sand. Determinedly she stood as erect as she could, looking up and down the beach, scanning every face. In my mind I could again see her face light up when the group of men who had rescued and then dehydrated Henry, came half leading and half carrying him up the beach. I could again see Henry's hangdog manner, with the showoff spirit completely gone, a deflated and uncertain man. And I could again see Lilly eagerly gather him into her arms.

Then that picture would be replaced by the mental picture of the rescuers. Their dark shirts and trousers wet with the spray or with sweat, their big chests still heaving from their exertions, modestly accepting the plaudits of the crowd that pressed around them. Again, as my mind reconstructed the scene, I was aware of the men's dark, coppery skins. Of course the color might be only from the wind and sun to which they were constantly exposed. But the cast of their features, combined with the bronze skin, suggested Indian blood, and I strongly suspected that they were Indians recruited from the nearby Reservation for Coast Guard service. If so, I thought, this was one more odd twist to this strange, eventful day: Red men risking their lives in a heroic rescue of Whites.

But most persistent of all, the one picture that recurred again and again and made me continue to toss restlessly in my bed, was the scene of that little rowboat being wrenched from my hands and rushed toward the river's seething funnel. I couldn't shut out the sight, nor my feeling as I watched the little man futilely trying to row against the current, and inevitably being borne toward what I was sure was the couple's doom. My eyes would pop open to shut out the sight. I couldn't relax enough even to begin to go to sleep.

Shirley, aware of my plight, finally spoke. "L'il old trailer gets us into things, doesn't it?"

In non-professorial language I replied, "And how!" Then, after a while, I added. "Strange! All my early years I longed for some adventure but couldn't find it. Now when you and I are old, Maggie, we're finding plenty."

"Not much of it quite so exciting as that you had today," said Shirley.

"Thank heaven, no!" I replied. "This kind of adventure is a bit too high-flying for my blood."

"High adventure on a low budget," said Shirley.

CHAPTER VI

OUR ROLLING VILLAGE VISITS MEXICO

We rounded a bend in the mountain road and caught our first glimpse of the river shimmering far below. It was close to midnight and we were in darkness except for the light from the waning moon and a row of bonfires along the river bank. The flickering beams from the fires made weird crawling creatures of the strange craft which plied from one bank to the other.

Following the tail light of the vehicle ahead, we worked our way down the winding descent. Finally rounding a low hill, we were at the top of the last steep drop to the turbulent stream toward which we had been working our way for the last fourteen hours.

It had been about ten o'clock that morning when we joined the long line of autos and house trailers which constituted our party. All the rest of the day and half the night we had spent inching our way toward this flooded Piaxtla River in western Mexico.

Facing that last drop to the swirling water, the sight was not reassuring. Mexican laborers, their trousers rolled to their hips, were working in the shallow water at the river's edge, helping the awkward contraptions which were being used as "ferries," to land and push off. This closer inspection did not make the huge grotesque shadows on the lead-colored water look any more inviting. It was but small comfort to realize that a couple of hundred trailers had already crossed ahead of us, and that at least an equal number stretched out for miles behind. Nor were we greatly consoled by the fact that most of the other adventurers were about as old as we were. At that minute we felt that all of us were old enough to know better.

Here on the ledge at the top of the last precipitous drop, we were brought to a halt. Mr. Ulysses, carrying a megaphone, raised a restraining hand. One of the little band of volunteer trailerists who were acting as his assistants, stepped over to our car. "Just a minute," he said; "wait till we see which ferry to put you on."

Roads which were little more than trails branched off to the right and left, and the trailers were being sent down one or the other of these. The main road which led to the larger ferry directly ahead was not for us. That was being used exclusively by the regular traffic — the Mexican buses loaded with men, women, and children, and sometimes goats, sheep, chickens, and even pigs; the trucks laden with cattle, grain, and farm produce; and the overcrowded autos, mostly of ancient vintage. All day long our trailers had been kept in

Trailering is a Karr family tradition. Here my father, Reverend Norman C. Karr, and my mother are preparing to leave their home in Lapeer, Michigan, for a trip to California to visit us in this early-type "expando" trailer (1926).

WAY BACK WHEN

Our trailer #1, a "Teardrop" (about 1932), was just big enough to sleep one and one-half persons in comfort. My son Norman and I used it for trout fishing in the California mountains.

Our trailer #2, a 16-foot Invader, gave us most of the essential comforts. In it our family toured the West Coast.

From our Montreal camp we could watch the great ocean-going ships plying their way to the Great Lakes cities on the newly opened St. Lawrence Seaway.

AND THEN THERE WAS CANADA...

The Royal Mounted Police were always helpful. In Ottawa, following the elaborate ceremony of *The Changing of the Guard*, Shirley converses with one of the Mounties.

Wide-spreading shade trees and spacious lawns provided a pleasant bivouac on Prince Edward Island.

The jeep station wagon that served as caboose, and back of us the other outfit we pulled through Kicking Horse Pass.

These "sky-high" fishermen erect their nets on dry ground, ready for the tidal bore to bring them a crop of fish!

. . . and the phenomenon of THE BIG BORE

Sometimes it is called "horse-and-wagon" fishing.

The tidal bore has brought in its fish and then receded, leaving the ground dry for the harvesting of the crop.

Tourists arrive a few minutes ahead of scheduled time, and wait for the tidal bore to come surging in from the ocean.

WE CALL IT SHANGRI-LA

It is pleasant to write *about* the outdoors while *in* the outdoors!

Neighbors help me build a large cabaña—our latest improvement—on our wood plot. Fortunately, our Shangri-La is situated in a community where genuine old-fashioned neighborliness still exists.

We found our end-of-the-rainbow in a grove of spruce trees north of Spokane. Here fellow trailerists, the Nattresses, stop off on their way from California to Vancouver Island, B.C.

MEXICO

Caravaners (on rock at left) watch the famous daredevil high dive at El Mirador Hotel, Acapulco.

In Zacatecas our caravan was bivouacked in the city's central park.

At a Sunday morning religious service, music was provided by an organ carried in one of the large trailers.

MEXICO

CONTINUED

The pink marble cathedral in San Miguel de Allende.

Crossing the flooded Piaxtla River on hastily prepared ferries—little more than rafts. Our turn came in the middle of the night. (Chet Coffee photo)

Magnificent Avenida del Mar (Ocean Drive) extends for miles along Mazatlan's waterfront.

Beach scene near the trailer park in Mazatlan where we have spent a part of each winter recently.

Trailers are parked under coconut palms. Coconuts are free.

The pool is used extensively by the trailerists. The water is pure, fresh, and filtered.

The lots are spacious, the grass is green, and the breezes gentle. Our No. 58 finds a pleasant berth here.

Upon getting acquainted with some of the desert mobile home parks our reaction was: "More laughter—not the kind that comes from bottles at so much a fifth—than we had heard in years!"

In traveling, the folding table and chairs from the trailer came in handy for out-door eating and relaxing.

Our son Norman (Dr. Norman W. Karr) and family are avid trailerists. Here they are camped at Lake George in the Sierras.

Our first retirement home was this 37-foot mobile home under date palms in a Palm Springs park. Here our daughter Kay is visiting us. (Photo by Roy Avery, Kay's husband.)

CANADA

Spectacular mountain scenery along the coast-to-coast Canadian Highway.

The late Wally Byam, one of the most dynamic and unconventional leaders who ever lived, whoops it up down Calgary's Main Street at the 1954 Stampede (1954 Caravan to Western Canada).

The Kamloops Chamber of Commerce brings their portable cooking outfit to our caravan bivouac in the city park to serve us a feast of delicious Kamloops trout (1954 caravan).

In the Quebec area, practically all signs are printed in both English and French. Here the author inspects a plaque commemorative of the French and English War for possession of Canada.

Local Indians stage an exhibition
for caravaners at Banff, B.C.

Young members of the 1959 caravan to Eastern Canada gather low-bush huckle-
berries (blueberries?) in our camp in one of Canada's many provincial parks.

Evening hush and serenity settles upon our camp in a Western Canada mountain meadow.

Wally Byam confers with the Royal Mountie who guided our 1954 caravan through a stretch of unfinished mountain road not open to the general public—the scene of your author's "moment of truth" as "caboose" for the caravan.

A caravaner pauses to **bar**ter with vendors in Mexico's famous center of silver artistry, Taxco.

MEXICO

At practically every rendezvous through Mexico the local citizens stage a celebration with entertainment for our enjoyment.

Art Costello, now President of Airstream Company, arranges to take his family on the San Blas Jungle Trip, 1955 caravan to Mexico.

Amidst Xochimilco's world-famous floating gardens, with canoe-and-barge-borne flower vendors offering arms full of bouquets at ridiculously low prices.

One of Mexico's many pyramids left by an early Indian culture.

Two of Mexico's many moods. Here are depicted music, dance, laughter—the gayety of the Mexican people. And **here** the solemnity and reverence of the magnificent cathedrals.

line at one side of the road crawling slowly ahead or stalled completely, while these local vehicles had gone blithely by. This arrangement — which had caused some grumbling among the trailerists — we
now learned from the volunteer traffic man at our car window, was
not upon the insistence or even the suggestion of the Mexican
officials. It was part of the caravan's effort to further the good
neighbor policy. Any budding resentment on our own part at this
Alphonse-and-Gaston act was quickly dispelled when our informant
told us that Mr. Ulysses and he, and other members of the parking
committee, had been on the job all the night before and all day, taking only a few minutes off during the small hours of the morning to
snatch a bit of sleep, when the Mexican laborers had refused to work
any longer without their *reposo*.

The main ferry, we were informed, had been set up by the
Mexican road commission to meet the emergency. Normally the river
was easily fordable (while there was a fine new paved highway all
the way to Mexico City, some of the bridges were not yet completed), but the flood had made it impassable except by ferry. The
"ferries" we were using were extemporized affairs that Ulysses had
somehow dug up.

"If we all took turns along with the local traffic, on just the
official ferries," said the tired trailerist at our window, "some of us
would be here till the middle of next week...Besides," he added,
"these trucks and buses mean bread and butter to these people. But
we," he smiled, "don't have to get anywhere, any time."

Just then Mr. Ulysses raised his megaphone and sang out, "Another
ferry ready." And we saw one of those fantastic carriers crawling up
to the rickety dock over to our left.

"How long is your trailer?" asked our friend at the window.

"Sixteen feet."

"Then you wait for the next ferry," said he. "This one will carry
a longer outfit. "Let the next fellow through." He motioned toward
the trail to our right. "Pull down there," he said. "Your ferry will be
along directly."

Soon our turn came. Saying our prayers, and crossing our fingers
too for good measure, we bumped our way down the steep incline.
The "dock" when we reached it, was merely a small platform floating
on barrels. Two swarthy little men sitting on the edge of the platform
smiled at us reassuringly. But a minute later they jumped to attention. Our "ferry" was coming in.

The "critter" which slipped eerily out of the darkness and
clumsily worked its way toward shore proved to be two dugout
canoes laced together with planks. Now it didn't look as big as it
had out on the water. In fact it looked small. Too small. But waved
forward by a smiling dark-skinned ferryman, we drove aboard. The
thing proved to be big enough, with maybe six inches to spare fore

and aft. The men on the barge adjusted the ropes (for this was a water-power ferry, manipulated by an ingenious arrangement of ropes and pulleys strung across the river so as to use the force of the current for propulsion), the bare-legged men on shore waded a few feet into the water to push us off, and we swung out onto the swirling river.

Once launched — as often happens with things that we dread and fear — the river did not seem nearly so wide or fearsome as it had from shore. In a surprisingly short time we were across the water and climbing the far bank. At the top we paused to look back. All were getting safely over. Later we learned that not a trailer was dunked. Not a person drowned. Not a tragedy. Just an exciting experience to remember.

The nearest approach to even a minor catastrophe happened next day, and was reported to us later. It proved to have humorous overtones. Trailerists were only indirectly involved — they had to get out of the way. It happened when a one-elephant-size circus pulled up to the main ferry to be transported. In the middle of the river the elephant either got scared or hilarious, or possibly just figured that this was too good an opportunity to pass up. At any rate, he tipped over the ferry.

The water was just deep enough for him to touch his toes to the bottom. He went part floating, part swimming, and part wading down the stream, passing uncomfortably close to one of the trailers. He liked the water so well that for a time he refused to be coaxed out. The only inconvenience to the trailerists was the wait while all hands turned in to help round up the elephant when he landed on shore a few hundred feet below the ferry crossing.

Meanwhile, Shirley and I had gone on to the next bivouac, which was a large field on the shore of the ocean in Mazatlan. There the scattered units of our city-on-wheels assembled to continue our hegira to San Blas, Guadalajara, Toluca, Lake Patzcuaro, Mexico City, Cuernavaca, Taxco, Acapulco, and back to Mexico City where we disassembled. But not that fast. Altogether our excursion in Mexico lasted about six weeks.

This was Mr. Ulysses' 1955 caravan to Mexico. Shirley and I had found so much pleasure in the 1954 caravan to Western Canada that we could not resist this call to Old Mexico.

When we crossed the border at Nogales, the welcoming ceremonies had been elaborate. The Mexican Government had postponed opening a new border gate pending our arrival. The ribbon-cutting function was performed by Governor Soto of Sonora, Mexico, and Governor McFarland of Arizona. Our caravan was ushered over the international line to the accompaniment of music played by a Mexican band, and the cheers and hand waves of a friendly populace. Schools had been let out for our passing, and sidewalks, fences, porches, and even telephone poles were loaded with children as well as adults. The children practiced their version of American speech on us, "A-lo, A-lo," accompanied by the most amiable grins imaginable; the adults called "Adios," that term meaning, we learned, both "Hello" and "Goodbye."

Four hundred and eighty-seven trailers constituted our rolling village; a roving community of well over a thousand persons. That was a bigger population than lived in most of the Michigan towns where I spent my boyhood. It was a lot of people to be living together on the move. I suspect that it may have been the largest aggregation of tourists ever to enter a foreign country at one time — that is, on a peaceful mission. Our country sent a somewhat larger group of "tourists" across the Mexican border on two previous occasions. But they were not engaged in the peaceful pursuit of pleasure as were we. And they were not welcomed as we were.

Our mass visit to Mexico had seemed significant enough to *Life* Magazine for them to send two photographers along as far as Guaymas. There they flew overhead and took pictures of our encampment with the trailers arranged in the pattern of concentric circles which constituted our regular setup. But the thing which impressed upon me the size of our ambulant village most vividly occurred that night. After a bonfire and songfest held in the "commons" at the center of the circle, a group of us chanced to be walking home together. In one of the aisles between rows of trailers we came upon a bewildered trailerist.

"Say," he inquired, "can you tell me where I am? These trailers all look so much alike I can't tell one from the other. I'm not kidding you, I'm lost."

Fortunately some of us had the lay of the land well enough in mind to help him out of his predicament.

Our village had, in addition to the individual trailers, two public establishments: (1) our post office and (2) our public baths. The latter had two showers for men and two for women, with generator to provide hot water. These baths were for the use of those who did not carry their own facilities. The bath and the post office were housed in one big trailer.

Our village population came from all over our nation and parts of Canada. There was even a Volkswagen bus from France with lettering on the side announcing that the occupants — the man a photographer for a French pictorial magazine — had traveled in their bus in Egypt, Alaska, and various other distant parts of the world. We had lawyers, doctors, dentists, nurses, farmers, teachers, merchants, salesmen, and representatives of many other occupations. That is, our village's citizens *had* filled all these jobs. Now, most of them were retired. Not all, by any means; we had both young and middle-aged people, including one young couple with a baby. But due to the length of our trip, the majority were older persons who had finished their labors; their time was their own and they didn't have to hurry home. That is an essential condition for the most complete enjoyment of such a jaunt as ours, not to feel hurried. Especially in Mexico. It's a shame to go to this pleasant land, where life moves at a slower, calmer tempo than here, and carry along one's subservience to a feverish time schedule.

Once through Nogales and on the open highway it was surprising how quickly the caravaners got scattered. Often we could not see a single trailer either ahead or behind us. We learned that five hundred trailers actually can travel without interfering too much with local traffic. To avoid congestion we made it a rule that never more than two of our outfits were to travel close together, except of course when we were convoyed. The only trouble was that, traveling spread out as we were, it took our procession a long time to pass a given point. The Mexican farmers working in the fields along the route didn't get much work done that day, since they always took time out to wave at each of us as we passed.

As our caravan glided smoothly over the paved highway, I could not help but think of another "caravan" that had passed this way almost two centuries before. For this was the very route over which Father Serra plodded, on foot and burro-back, to found the chain of missions up and down the length of California. What a contrast! Here we were, riding on air-cushioned tires, our little traveling home, although only 16 feet long, containing all the essential comforts and conveniences of 20th-Century living.

Our first overnight stop was in Hermosillo, 186 miles south of the Nogales border. The caravan camped in an open field next to a handsome modern trailer park, which of course was far too small to accommodate our crowd.

Provisions for sanitation had been made. And our own sanitation committee, headed by one of our doctors, saw to it that the sanitary facilities were kept sanitary. Electricity was provided, not enough for individual trailers but sufficient to light our camp. Pure bottled water, bottled gas, ice, baked goods, *cerveza* (beer) and groceries were sold from wagons at our doors. Gasoline was one thing that had given me unnecessary concern. It was well taken care of. In Mexico the gasoline business is owned and operated by the government, and the government sent an official ahead of us the entire length of our route, seeing that there was an abundant supply of gasoline waiting for us at every city and town. We never lacked. However, in the smaller towns the extra supply had to be stored in barrels, and the stations literally "rolled out the barrel" to welcome us.

On the second day in Hermosillo, Shirley and I pulled our trailer out of camp and rented a space in the modern trailer park next door

— on doctor's orders. Shirley had developed a distressful rash over her body on the way to Nogales (probably caused by the shots taken in preparation for the trip). Dr. Val St. John, a courtly, European-trained, retired surgeon from British Columbia, who acted as one of our caravan's physicians — all without fee —suggested that a tub bath in lukewarm water in which a box of soda had been dissolved would help to relieve the itching, and advised us to get into the trailer park and use one of their handsome marble baths. We made the shift. Then I went downtown to a *tienda de aborrotes* (grocery store) to get the soda. There I had a brush with the Spanish language. To the smiling dark-skinned proprietress I said, "A box of soda, please."

"Si, si, señor. Soda." She went to a metal chest containing cracked ice and fished out a bottle of poisonous-looking green liquid. She started to wipe off the bottle on a towel.

"No, no," I said. "Not that. I want powder, p-o-w-d-e-r." I spelled out the word and talked a little louder, giving labored attention to my articulation, trying to make her understand.

She looked blank. "No want?" she said, pointing to the bottle, "Ees soda."

I shook my head. I looked over the shelves but could see nothing resembling our soda packages. So I indicated by gestures that I would leave and come back. She smiled and nodded. I drove back to the trailer and got out our Spanish dictionary. *Bicarbonato*, said the dictionary. I hurried back to the store and said to the lady, *"bicarbonato."*

"O-o-o-h," said she, and came from behind the counter, took me by the arm and led me to the door. There she pointed to a store up the street a few doors and across the way. It had a sign *Botica* over the front. *"Botica,"* said she, and then repeated, *"botica o farmacia."* She gave me a gentle, friendly push in that direction.

At the drugstore I bought soda in little folded papers like old fashioned headache powders, at ten *centavos* (less than one cent in our money) a powder. I bought out practically her whole stock — which I imagined consisted of one or two packages of our soda divided up into these tiny "powders." It proved to be good medicine. Next day Shirley's misery was relieved. We went on with the caravan.

At Guaymas, famous old port and fishing village, we laid over an extra day for the fishermen in our party to wet a line.

At Navajoa we left the paved highway to visit the charming, old-world-like town of Alamos. Here, at one time, silver bullion mined in the surrounding hills was brought to be minted into coins. The coins were shipped to Spain to keep the proud Spanish Armada dominant on the seas. That was before the Pilgrims landed at Plymouth Rock.

At Culiacan we encountered rain. Rain, we were assured, was "most unseasonable"; nevertheless it came down in sheets. Lasting intermittently for several days, the rain could have been dispiriting.

But the local citizens laid themselves out to keep our spirits up. They opened all the private clubs for our use, gave fiestas in public buildings, furnished guides to show us the sights, and did what they could to make us forget the inclement weather.

Here Shirley and I had our first — and only — experience in being entertained by a governor. Along with Mr. Ulysses and twenty or thirty other caravaners we chanced to be invited to the mansion of Governor Pico for a luncheon. Neither the governor nor his beautiful wife—I do not use the adjective loosely—spoke a word of English. But it wasn't necessary. Some of the Mexican guests did speak English, and some of our group spoke Spanish. For the rest of us the warm hospitality of our hosts, the pleasant, flower-scented surroundings, the soft mariachi music, the delectable luncheon, offered an acceptable substitute for a common language.

The rain caused rivers to swell and held us in Culiacan for a week. And our departure, when it came, was accomplished with the scalp-tingling excitement I recounted earlier.

Mazatlan is a sightly city on the coast. Our parking lot was a field next to the sea. Driving down the lane that led to our encampment, I came upon a car stopped in the road with a man standing beside it. Inwardly I expressed my feelings toward thoughtless people who stop to visit in the middle of the road. I pulled out and started to go round. The man beside the car stepped in front of us and held up his hand. He didn't have on his blue beret, the distinguishing mark of the caravaners, and I didn't recognize him as one of our parking committee. He began to cuss us for being impatient. We cussed back. (I'm using the editorial *we*; Shirley didn't participate.)

"What's your damned hurry?" said he.

"What t'hell you blocking the road for?"

"Can't you read?"

"Read what?"

"Why, that sign," said he, pointing to a sign directly in front of the other car where I couldn't see it with him blocking it off.

Now I saw that the sign read: "Parking fee 25 cents a night." He was collecting the fee. Tempers were running short, after the long rain. Knowing the hard, self-sacrificing work the parking committee had been doing, I apologized, taking all the blame. I was forgiven. The breach was healed.

With respect to this collecting of fees, it was our practice to make such collections at each of our stops (though not usually in the middle of a lane). When the village or city did not levy a fee for our electricity, we would donate the amount to some deserving charity of the mayor's selection. The local papers gave considerable favorable publicity to this gesture of friendliness.

In our parking lot there at Mazatlan, Shirley and I were entertained by an unexpected and unscheduled event, a bit of monkey business. We were parked against a fence at one edge of the field. Directly beyond the fence was a house and yard. In the yard, between two trees, was a large monkey tethered on a sliding chain. We were getting settled in our trailer when from the direction of the monkey came an unearthly screech. We hurried out to see what was happening. The monkey had a cat up one of the trees and was putting it through what appeared to be some sort of initiation ceremony. The monkey was hanging head down with his tail wrapped around a limb of the tree. In one paw he was holding the cat's tail, with the cat hanging head down too, but trying to claw its way upright. The cat was protesting with all the strength of its lungs, and the monkey was appearing to enjoy the racket. He swung the cat back and forth, then tossed it upward and caught it by a paw. He swung it that way for a while, with the cat trying to reach up and claw him but not quite being able to reach. All this time the cat was screeching wildly. To no avail. It was only when the monkey decided that it was time to conclude the ceremony that the cat got any relief, and then only after the monkey had caught him by the scuff of the neck and carried him down from the tree.

Our social committee scheduled a banquet at Mazatlan's luxurious Hotel Belmar — the hotel long famous for a pet python which, according to reports, used to roam the halls. It is dead now and, again according to reports, preserved in alcohol. We did not see it. The banquet was quite sumptuous. One item on the menu was venison. Near us someone asked, "How do you say venison in Spanish?"

Across the table sat Don Forsythe, a slender, quiet fellow with a sly sense of humor. Having in mind the half-wild little burros that roam the hills, Don replied, "Burro, spelled b-u-r-r-o!"

As usual we had lovely slender senoritas as well as a bespangled mariachi band to entertain us. But for us, as entertaining as anything was the impromptu dance participated in by some of our group. Two of our caravaners were the Burke twins, handsome young men about twenty-one years old; they with their parents were taking a winter holiday from a large northern wheat farm. The boys are not the forward type; but some more aggressive caravaner, seeing the possibility of international harmonizing, got the girls' ears and set them up to "shanghai" the modest, self-effacing young men. The girls literally pulled them out of their chairs. Once on the floor the boys proved to be good dancers, quick to learn Spanish dance steps under the girls' instruction. Fine entertainment. But the best entertainment, for me at least, was what we saw when we left the hotel. Directly in front of the entrance is the ocean. The phosphorous-tipped waves breaking against the wall made broad, undulating sheets of shimmering lights, a scene of incomparable beauty, not soon to be forgotten.

On the way to the seacoast town of San Blas we began to get the feel of the tropics. Dense forests lined the highway; here and there thatch-roofed houses in clearings suggested the South Sea Islands; parrots winged overhead, their bright feathers glinting in the sun; and as we got nearer the ocean we saw large banana and cocoanut plantations. This was Sunday and in and near the tiny villages people lined the highways to wave at us, the men all wearing their Sunday best, gleaming white cotton suits; and the women wearing colorful native dresses. One wondered how the men's suits could be so white when they are washed only by woman-power beating them against rocks along the shores of streams and ponds.

San Blas is rich in history. But now it is just a sleepy fishing village. The citizens of San Blas joined the caravaners in staging a rollicking dance — a hybrid affair, half Mexican folk dances, half old-fashioned American square dances — in which everybody joined. It was good fun.

On the highway beyond San Blas our auto was seized with an indisposition. Apparently peevish from the frequent dips and rises in altitude from sea level to mountain tops, it stopped dead, belching steam. This was miles away from any town or garage. In a few minutes along came a caravaner. He pulled off the road and came back to look under the hood with me; but apparently he was no more able to diagnose the nature of the ailment than I. All he could do was cluck his sympathy. Then came another caravaner. His look under the hood was with understanding. Working with wrench, screwdriver, and intelligence, he soon had our carburetor off and apart, then back together again, and the machine functioning with its old-time vigor. He appeared a little offended at our offer of compensation.

Such acts of mutual helpfulness occur frequently on a caravan. I emphasize this to make it clear that the heated verbal exchange in Mazatlan was an exception, not the rule.

Of all the cities I know, Guadalajara is one of the most appealing — particularly because of the surrounding country: charming small towns like Ajijic, Tlaquepaque, and Lake Chapala, where native Indian crafts flourish. But to us caravaners, the city is most notable for its hospitality. No city could lay itself out more openhandedly to welcome a band of visitors.

At the first big fiesta in our honor, staged by the Guadalajara Lions' Club, not only were we welcomed by the governor of the state and the mayor of the city, we had the added honor of being greeted by the American Consul, Mr. F. L. Lineweaver.

In the social gathering after the speech-making, I chanced to be standing next to the local Chamber of Commerce representative who had acted as master of ceremonies. Since he spoke English, of a sort, I engaged him in conversation. I asked him what he really thought of the caravan. He replied with what appeared to be genuine enthusiasm, mentioning particularly what it meant to have us place our aluminum homes next to their adobe and stone ones, and really come to know their people. Thinking of the possibility of writing an article expressing some of my thoughts on the significance of these caravans, I asked him, "Will you write some of that down for me?" Using the back of an envelope, this is what he wrote: "Your caravan do more in the good willing of two peoples than many official ambassador."

And, while on the subject of "good willing," I'll repeat a somewhat similar testimony from a United States citizen whom we ran across in Morelia. On the steps of one of the hotels, a tall dignified *norte-americano* spotted Shirley and me, in our blue berets. He stepped over and introduced himself. He was, we learned, a doctor of medicine doing extensive research on certain viruses which are prevalent in Mexico. His name, which at his request I am withholding, is well known in medical circles in our country. "Your caravan," he volunteered, "from the standpoint of mutual understanding between the people of Mexico and the people of the United States, is the greatest thing that ever hit Mexico."

While in Guadalajara three minor events occurred which were entertaining and perhaps significant. All three happenings were phases of our bouts with the Spanish language. Incidentally, they are the type of thing that caused Shirley and me to take Spanish lessons when we got back home, in prepartion for our successive trips to Mexico.

Ross Frasher, retired principal of a Los Angeles high school, and his wife Mary, took us sightseeing in their car. When we stopped at a gasoline station the young Mexican attendant looked Ross up and down and asked in broken English, "You Gringo?"

"No," said Ross, using the big engaging grin which helped to make him a popular school administrator. "United States citizen, *norte-americano*." Then he made his smile even broader and added, "You Greaser?"

The young Mexican got the point. His grin matched Ross's. "No Greaser," he said. "Mexican." Then he added something significant. Pointing to Ross and then to himself, he said, "*Amigos*" (friends).

Next morning a gold inlay came out of one of my teeth. Looking over the buildings I saw a sign *Dentista* and climbed the steps to the office. The young dentist welcomed me amiably but spread his hands and shrugged to indicate that he did not speak English. I showed him the filling and the hole in the tooth. He nodded, "*Si, si*," and ushered me to a chair.

To my gratification he scrubbed his hands vigorously and thoroughly before cementing in my filling. Then, after keeping my mouth propped open a jaw-tiring length of time, he undertook to tell me what I should do about eating. Having had other inlays cemented in I knew pretty well what he was trying to tell me; but having struggled through numerous attempts to make myself understood to Mexicans, I took perverse pleasure in letting him labor through his instructions. I could practically see his brains at work on the problem. At last he held his hand in front of my face, the four fingers bunched to indicate my upper jaw and the thumb serving as my lower jaw. With laborious precision he said, "*H-o-y m-e-d-i-o-d-i-a*,"—he paused long enough to see that I understood, "today noon." Then quickly and forcefully he brought the fingers and thumb together in a fair simulation of vigorous eating, and giving his head a vigorous shake of negation, added, "No, no, no!" After pausing to make sure from my affirmative nod that I understood, he concluded, "*Hoy de noche* (today night)" — again he went through the energetic chop-chopping with his hand — "Okay, okay, okay!" People everywhere seem to have adopted our "okay."

The third event came near the end of our week's stay in Guadalajara. An elderly caravaner — who at one time had been a prominent political figure in California, we'll call him Arthur Breeden — sustained a fall. It was not a serious accident; he recovered in a few days. But meanwhile he suffered considerable pain in his back. Mexican visitors to our camp, solicitous for "Señor Breeden's" welfare, insisted that he must go to a hospital. They got on the phone and tried to have him admitted. But hospitals there are like hospitals here at home, pretty well filled. The only vacant bed they could locate was in a maternity hospital. Out of special consideration for the *norteamericanos*, Mr. Breeden was admitted there.

Since Mr. Breeden had once been a neighbor of ours in Palm Springs, Shirley and I went to call on him. We found him in good spirits, well cared for, and having fun over his admittance to a maternity hospital.

Back at camp we reported the accident to mutual friends of Arthur's and ours, Vera and Ed Ferris from Florida. Next day they went to call on him. The hospital being located near the heart of the city, visitors have to go through the center of Guadalajara to get to it. At a main intersection Ed leaned out of the window to ask directions of a traffic officer, naming the maternity hospital. Ed and Vera, by the way, are a youngish couple, else the following sequence of events might not have occurred. The officer glanced into the car and saw Vera. He jumped from the pedestal where he had been directing traffic, rushed to the side of the street where his motorcycle was parked, climbed aboard and turned on the siren, waving to the Ferrises and shouting something they interpreted to mean "Follow me!"

Leaving the corner traffic to take care of itself, with siren screeching the motorcycle officer led the Ferrises swiftly, and noisily, to the hospital.

Inside the hospital the sound of the approaching siren galvanized a doctor and a hospital official into action. They rushed to the door and down the steps. When Ed calmly stepped out and announced that they were there to see "Señor Breeden," the Mexican hospital officials at first looked bewildered, then burst into hearty laughter. They shook hands all the way round at the good joke.

In such a hurried, butterfly-like touching upon the highlights of our trip, what shall I leave out of our itinerary? Shall it be Mexico City, which many — with some justice, I think — consider to be the handsomest city on our continent? Shall it be the Aztec ruins? Beautiful Lake Patzcuaro? Toluca, Taxco, Morelia, Uruapan? Shall it be Acapulco? Surely not Acapulco.

Acapulco was the grand climax of our safari; from there we broke up into small groups for the trip home, some by way of Laredo, some by way of El Paso, and some by way of Nogales. Not a few of the caravaners found Acapulco so fascinating that they stayed on for weeks after the caravan had broken up. And why not? Take a halfmoon bay of sky-blue water surrounded by the warmest, softest sand imaginable. Take a climate so gentle that the caravaners could, and did, go swimming at midnight as well as midday. Take all the superlatives of all the city boosters and roll them into one and extract their essence . . . that's how Acapulco impressed many of us.

Now, after the above effulgence, in the interest of honest reporting I have to say that I do not recommend that you drop everything and run not walk to Acapulco, with the expectation of finding never-ending perfection on earth. Recently I talked to a friend who says that when he went to Acapulco he couldn't get out of there fast enough—too hot! Nevertheless, for Shirley and me the memory of a near-perfect week beckons us back with an irresistible allurement.

But, even more vivid than Acapulco is the memory of that exciting crossing of the swollen Piaxtla River. That experience is particularly vivid in our memories because to us it typifies the spirit of a trailer caravan. Perhaps an anecdote will illustrate: In those long waits there beside the highway — it took three full days, working almost around the clock, to get us all across the river — some caravaners got out their comfortable folding chairs and sat and read or chatted with neighbors; some used folding tables to stage impromptu beer and card parties; some took pictures; some lay on the comfortable beds in their trailers and slept. A few of the men dug up shotguns they had brought along — they had to obtain special permission at the border for this — and had good quail shooting in the surrounding woods. To make things as comfortable as possible we did not crawl along steadily; our traffic committeemen would let us stand in one spot sometimes for an hour or two at a time, before asking us to move.

I enjoyed watching the passing traffic. It was a cross section of

Mexico. There were overcrowded autos, mostly of ancient vintage, driven by smiling Mexicans. These alternated with the big and shiny cars usually (but not always) driven by *norteamericanos.* There were three types of buses, (1) first class: big and comfortable through buses not unlike passenger buses north of the border, (2) second class: older local buses which stopped at every crossroad, invariably overloaded with farmers' families and local citizens, (3) third class: old rattletraps — worn-out buses from class one and class two — loaded with the poorest peons. Likely the passengers on these third-class buses would be holding a sheep or a goat or a pig by a cord, or carrying a hen or a goose or a turkey in their arms. There were trucks, some as modern as tomorrow carrying produce to market, some old and worn and wobbly going from town to town or farm to farm. There was only one element lacking to make this traffic a true cross section of Mexico — because of the swollen river there were none of the trains of laden burros led by barefoot laborers, which are so plentiful throughout Mexico.

In one of those long waits between moves, Shirley went into the trailer and brought out the little electric organ she always carries with us — described in Chapter I. I started to unpack the duffel from around the electric generator in our trunk. To occupants of neighboring trailers who had gathered around to see what we were up to, Shirley said, "Soon's he gets the generator going we can have some community singing."

"Here," said the man from the trailer immediately back of us, "let me furnish the juice. We're all set up for it."

And they were. George and Mary Neetz, a hearty-looking couple full of smiles and laughter, did not look their seventy-five years. On their pickup truck they had not only the generator all primed and ready to go, but also a big spare tank of gasoline, a giant-size water tank, and a bountiful supply of canned stuff ready for extended travel.

"For forty-three years," said George Neetz, "I was a Ford dealer in Illinois. But wife and I always wanted to travel. I never sold a car that I didn't wish I could get into it and go and go and keep on going. So when I retired a few years back, it didn't take us long to get going. I rigged up this truck with light plant and a big tank of water to have along for spare, bought this twenty-six foot trailer, and we set out. And we just about do what we always thought we'd like to do, just keep on going. Here's an example: on July 4, 1953, we were in Vancouver, B.C.; on February 4, 1954 we were in Key West, Florida; on July 4, 1954 we were in Halifax, Nova Scotia; now in February 1955 here we are in Mexico." And then he added with heartfelt enthusiasm, "What a life!"

I guess that little extemporized songfest there on the Mexican highway was about as memorable an experience as any we had on

this caravan. The way the passing Mexicans showed their appreciation and their sympathetic understanding, was heartwarming. Their
smiles, and bows, and clapping of hands make pleasant memory
pictures in our minds.

Mexico is a land of much poverty. But it is also a land of music —
of smiles, and laughter, and music. It is a happy land. And our songfest there beside the highway struck a responsive chord in Mexican
hearts.

The little spontaneous songfest also represents the spirit of a
trailer caravan.

CHAPTER VII

THE BULLFIGHT THAT WAS DIFFERENT

The bullfight was staged just for us. No one else came because no one else was invited. It was a good thing nobody else did come for they couldn't have found seats. There were over four hundred in our party, enough to fill this private stadium to its utmost capacity.

By *us* I mean the members of our 1957 trailer caravan to Mexico. We had crossed the border at El Paso a few days before and were now being entertained at a noted hacienda north of Mexico City. The chief business of the hacienda was raising fighting bulls, with the entertainment of paying guests a side line.

Many of us were at the bull ring not exactly under duress, but certainly in a state of squeamish uncertainty, dominated by the feeling that we probably shouldn't be there. We'd been induced by a promise. The owner of the hacienda, whom I'll call Señor de Silva, had given a reception for us upon our arrival the previous afternoon. Gathered in the high-vaulted hall in the great stone mansion which we caravaners called the palace, and served numerous rounds of a concoction of orange juice well fortified with tequila, we were receptive to Señor de Silva's invitation and assurance.

Waiting until we had become well juiced, Señor de Silva then rose to speak. Tall, dignified, looking like a Spanish grandee, he addressed us in flawless English with no trace of accent. After the customary phrases of welcome, including the inevitable Mexican phrase *Es su casa* (this is your house), he extended two invitations, the first of which we accepted with alacrity and the second with misgivings.

"This evening," he said, "Señora de Silva and I would like to have you as our guests at a fiesta in the grove."

The "grove" was a park of flowering shade trees where birds sang and artistic stone paths were bordered with inviting iron-grill seats. I could not recall having seen any arrangements for cooking as Shirley and I strolled through the grove on the way to the reception, but that did not deter me from joining my fellows in their nods of approval of the idea.

"And," went on our host, "tomorrow morning we are staging a bullfight in your honor."

This time I did not detect any nods of approval. The general reaction was expressed by a man next to me who mumbled, "No bullfight for me. I simply couldn't take it, that's all."

Señor de Silva apparently knew his *norteamericanos* and was prepared for our lack of enthusiasm. "I know," he said, "many of you prefer the gentle sport football," he paused to favor us with a slow, expressive smile which held a touch of satire, "but we would like to have you become acquainted with the skill which a bullfighter must possess. To that end we have arranged a very special type of bullfight. Bloodshed will be held to an absolute minimum — probably not more than a good nosebleed at one of your prize fights." Again he paused for his gentle irony to sink in, and went on. "This much I promise you, no bull will be killed. I repeat, on the honor of the house of de Silva, not a single bull will be killed."

I noticed that he did not promise that no bull*fighter* would be killed. Apparently they had to take their chances.

The outdoor dinner that evening was like being on a Walt Disney movie set depicting a royal courtyard. The grove had been transformed into a bower of softly colored lights where the sweet music of mariachi bands soothed the ears and the odors of strange but enticing foods titillated the appetite. Temporary kitchens and dining areas had been set up at various stations throughout the grove. An order of progression was established and by easy stages we moved from one station to another, at each station being served exotic but delectable foods. The idyllic quality of the occasion was ruffled briefly at one station when an energetic caravaner who did all things precipitately, reached over and selected from a dish of appetizers a small Mexican white pepper. With his customary zeal he popped it into his mouth and chomped. This morsel, as most visitors to Mexico soon learn, is not meant to be chomped, especially not by *norteamericanos* who are unaccustomed to the excessive heat the tiny pepper generates. Our precipitous caravaner emitted a "whoosh! wow!" and grabbed for the stein of beer in front of him. When he got his breath he commented. "Tasted as if I had a swarm of bees in my mouth." For some time afterward his face continued flushed. Frequently he wiped sweat beads from his forehead and tears from his eyes, and then would use the handkerchief to fan his red face. Other than that the meal, we caravaners felt, was of the type and in a setting such as oriental potentates must enjoy.

Thus elaborately wined and dined, and with our prejudices at least partly tranquilized by Señor de Silva's assurances, the next morning we prepared to attend the bullfight *en masse*.

On the way to the bull ring we marvelled at the mile upon mile we drove over the rolling acres of the hacienda. It is worthy of note, illustrative of Mexican mores, while Mexico had been cutting up many of these vast estates and dividing the land among the peasants, this splendid domain had been left intact. Obviously the Mexicans, in spite of their enthusiasm for land reform, wanted no government interference with the raising of bulls to supply their bull rings.

One of the caravaners riding in the car with us grew dreamy-eyed. "Wouldn't you just *love* to live on an estate like this? Isn't this the life?"

Just then we passed an Indian village of mud huts, dogs, pigs, naked or half-naked children, and bedraggled women, where some of the workers of the ranch lived. A practical-minded man in our group looked appraisingly at the squalor and poverty and turned to answer the woman's question.

"It sure is the life," he said, "for the *haciendados* — that's the people up at the palace, if you don't happen to know — but if I'd been born into this life it'd been just my luck to be one of these Indians."

After we had driven ten or fifteen miles back from the highway and away from the "palace," the woman posed another question.

"Why in the world do they have the bull ring way back here? You'd think they'd put it up where people wouldn't have to drive so far."

"That's easy," replied the man who had answered before, "this is where the bulls are." And then continuing the questions and answers by himself he went on, "Question: And why are the bulls way back here? Answer: To prevent their being contaminated by contact with visitors like us. They want to keep their bulls wild."

I surmised that the man was right — that, plus the need of protecting the visitors from a bull that might chance to break through a fence.

Upon arriving at the ring we found it to be a miniature arena but complete in its appointments. Señor de Silva in his speech of welcome had informed us that a motion picture of the day, *The Brave One*, had been filmed in this arena. On one side was a small covered grandstand reserved for the de Silvas. It already was completely filled when we arrived. For the rest of us, bleachers extended all the way around the tiny amphitheater. The rows of steeply banked seats were filling rapidly. The planks that served as seats were narrow. The planks *below* the seats, intended to walk on and rest the feet on when we were seated, were narrower still — in fact downright skimpy. Some of the finest exhibitions of courage I saw in the arena that day were elderly ladies treading their precarious way along these narrow planks and determinedly making their way to vacant seats. I was proud of Shirley. In truth I was a little proud of me.

Glancing around the crowd of caravaners I was pleased to see Santa Claus — otherwise known as J. Conrad McPheeters of Crescent City, California. His portly frame, bushy snow-white whiskers, and happy countenance made him a perfect ringer for the jolly old gentleman from the North Pole. And he, apparently enjoying the part, played genial host to the hordes of Mexican children who swarmed around him almost constantly. Now, haunched upon the plank which was far too narrow for his plump rump, he was trying to draw up his knees to let fellow caravaners past to join friends beyond. The fact that they trampled upon his feet and brushed their elbows against his whiskers did not wipe the genial smile from his face. Possibly he considered it not too great a price to pay for a short respite from his childish admirers on the outside.

Down in the ring all was excitement. Many of the caravan's amateur photographers were snapping pictures like mad, the subjects being the bullfighters who were there in numbers. These fighters were not full-fledged professionals. They were pupils learning to be professionals. One of the purposes of the ring was to serve as a training ground for aspiring young fighters who lived at the ranch to complete their training. And a handsome lot of young men they were — Mexico's finest.

Shirley leaned over and pinched my arm. "Look there, Harrison."

"Look where?"

"Right there in front of your nose. Don't you see? It's that Francisco."

I located him, and Francisco it surely was. On the way home from the reception the day before this young fellow, built like Michelangelo's statue of David, had overtaken Shirley and me and instead of passing on by had stopped to give us a friendly greeting. To our considerable surprise he addressed us in good United States English.

"How long are you folk staying here at the hacienda?"

"Only till tomorrow," I replied, "but . . . tell me, how did you learn to use our language so well?"

His grin showed gleaming white teeth, their whiteness accentuated by his dark skin. "Oh," he said offhandedly, "I live up *close* to the United States. I'm from Texas . . . Permit me to introduce myself. I'm Francisco Villarreal from El Paso." And chuckling he went on past, leaving us wondering.

Now here he was having his picture snapped by our camera enthusiasts. Obviously he was one of the fighters.

Francisco, like the dozen or so other young fighters, was dressed in the traditional tight jacket and knee pants. But none of these young men sported the bespangled costumes depicted in bullfight posters. Their outfits were of sturdy material, strictly for service.

It became apparent that we were not to be treated to the parade, the strutting of a gold-braided majordomo, nor the other fanfare which customarily precedes a bullfight. Instead, after some milling around by officials and semi-officials, and much picture taking, our Mr. Ulysses strode to the center of the ring carrying his megaphone. He first introduced to us a young lady who was learning to be a bullfighter but who unfortunately was not fighting that day. Then he introduced us to the other fighters as a group. And with a flourish he announced, "The fight will now begin."

There was a scurrying of amateur photographers for exits. The fighters sauntered with ostentatious deliberateness to various barricades around the inside of the wall. A *picador* carrying a long pike rode a heavily padded and blindfolded horse into the arena and took his place near a wall. An expectant hush settled over the crowd.

A gate flew open and through it plunged a black animal. My first reaction was disappointment at the size of the bull. At Señor de Silva's reception I had noticed on a wall pictures of fighting bulls engaged in combat, and in the pictures they looked enormous — wild, fierce, and simply enormous. This fellow that rushed through the gate wasn't big, he was small. But with respect to the wildness and fierceness he looked as if he would fill the bill all right. His eyes were wild, his manner so aggressively defiant that I suspected he had been prodded into fury before the gate was thrown open to admit him. Inside the enclosure he paused momentarily, tossing his head this way and that as if trying to get his bearings in this new environment — or trying to locate somebody or something to attack. The gate latch clicked behind him and he swung around with lowered head, ready to charge. Seeing nothing, he turned back, scanning the arena with alert, fierce eyes. His stance was that of a pugilist poised for violent action. He pawed the dirt angrily, snorting defiance to the whole world. Lust for life was evident in his every movement. Lust for anybody's life!

A *banderillero* stepped from a barricade carrying his bundle of ribbon-bedecked darts. He waved the darts at the bull and the bull charged. The *banderillero* dodged back to safety before the bull could reach him.

The bull swung quickly around looking for more movement. At the far side of the arena another *banderillero* jumped from behind one barricade and scurried to another. The bull raced in pursuit. Barely had the *banderillero* reached the new island of safety when the bull arrived. The animal banged head-on into the heavy piles that guarded the barricade's entrance. Clear across the arena we could plainly hear the crash of the horns against the heavy timbers.

"*Caramba!*" exclaimed someone near us, "That collision would have knocked his brains out if he'd had any."

The jar didn't seem to faze the bull. He swung around, switched his tail, and glared about for another moving object. Small as he was he wasn't fooling for a single minute. He meant business, the business of killing. And the *banderilleros* — who no doubt were members of the group of young fighters in training — were cautious in showing themselves. One of them not far from the bull extended an arm through the barricade's opening and shook the darts, and drew a crashing charge from the infuriated animal. Throughout the fight the *banderilleros* used the darts only to threaten the bull, never to plunge into his neck as is done in ordinary bullfights; thus it appeared Señor de Silva was fulfilling his pledge to avoid needless bloodshed.

Now came a new phase of the fight. The *picador*, who had been sitting immobile and thus escaping the bull's notice, now kicked his horse into taking a few steps forward. Instantly the bull charged. Like a playground-size steam engine he rushed across the arena and slammed into the side of the horse. There he gouged and rooted, as if trying to get his horns under the horse's belly and pitch him over the wall. But the horse, being about twice as big as the bull, was not easily pitched. I wondered, however, how long it would be before the bull found a vulnerable spot in the horse's padding and disemboweled him. A *banderillero* came into the open and shouted and waved to attract the bull's attention. The bull took after him, but when he disappeared behind his shelter the bull turned back to his vendetta with the horse. The *picador*, taking care to lift his foot well out of the danger zone, simply let the bull gore; and the well-padded horse likewise appeared not too greatly disturbed by the attack — possibly being simply too old and tired and inured to this kind of treatment to care. From time to time the bull would step back a pace or two as if sizing up the horse in an effort to devise *some way* to hoist the big lug over the fence. Then he would plunge back to the attack. He wasn't easily discouraged.

One of the caravaners near us cracked, "Who's fighting the bull, the men or the horse?"

"Nobody's fighting the *bull*," replied a man nearby, a man who had the tanned color of someone who spent much time outdoors, perhaps on a ranch. "It isn't a *bull*. It's a *cow*."

A cow? I looked closer. Although lacking the noticeable appendage of a giver of milk — indeed lacking any noticeable appendage that might be revealing — there undoubtedly was an embryonic something to convince me that this man knew his bovines. A cow! Hmmm! That could account for the animal's smallness. But what about its fierceness? This certainly was not representative of the "gentler" sex. It was a long long way from the contented cows our ads proclaim. Fantastic! This breeding of a race of cattle where even the females had just one purpose in life, a lust to commit mayhem. Oh ho! I thought, so that's what de Silva meant. No *bulls* would be killed. Just *cows*. Why the . . . ! My thoughts became unprintable.

But our informant was going on. "Don't think for a single minute that because these are cows you won't get your money's worth. These babies are tough. Plenty young fighters would rather fight a bull than one of these heifers. They've got a better chance to dodge. Bulls close their eyes when they charge; cows keep theirs open."

Now this heifer was in another of her brief moments of cogitation. She had backed off a few paces and was apparently trying again to devise some new plan of attack. The *picador*, evidently feeling that there was danger of her getting wearied of her fruitless efforts, reached out with his pike and jabbed her in the shoulder. Her response was quick and savage. With renewed ferocity she banged into the horse.

"At'a baby!" exclaimed our informant. "If she didn't have the right stuff in her she wouldn't have come back after that jab ... You know de Silva has a reason for fighting these heifers. It ain't all just to entertain us."

At that minute there came another distraction. For the first time since the show began a *matador* — the fellow who does the actual bull killing — entered the ring. Now it comes! I thought. Guess we're in for it.

To my not very great surprise the young fellow was our Francisco; somehow he had impressed me as a young man who would be in the front of any group or situation. He approached the cow from the rear walking carefully and quietly. When he got within a few feet of the animal he stopped, extended his cape out to one side and held it rigidly. He got himself set in the position he wanted. The stands grew hushed in anticipation. The *banderilleros* who had cautiously advanced a few feet from their barricades in an effort to distract the cow from the attack upon the horse, now withdrew. All eyes were centered upon Francisco — all except the cow's; she was still concentrating upon her effort to hoist the horse over the wall.

Francisco was a striking figure as he stood poised, alert, watching the cow's every move. He seemed the embodiment of grace and strength perfectly in balance. For one brief instant I experienced something of the thrill the Mexicans appear to feel at these spectacles.

Francisco shouted. The cow whirled. But since Francisco stood absolutely immobile the cow seemed unsure of the source of the sound. Francisco gave the red cape — the single item of bright color in his costume or his accouterment — a little shake. The cow lunged. Without moving his body Francisco swung the cape smoothly ahead of the cow's horns until she went thundering past. By the time the animal had turned and was ready for the return trip Francisco had shifted the cape to his other side. There he repeated in reverse the process of leading the animal past.

While the cow gathered herself for a repeat performance, Francisco took a few steps backward. Moving thus between rushes he lured the cow to the center of the ring. There Francisco took his stand and led the cow through his repertoire: the *veronicas*, the *recortes*, and the other fancy maneuvers which we read of and which mean so much to rabid bullfight fans. To this unitiated audience the perfection of Francisco's technique, or lack of it, meant little. To a young bullfighter who had gone through months and even years of training and was now perhaps for the first time performing before the public, what a disappointing audience we must have been. From us came none of the coveted *ole's* of approval. Not even a hiss of disapproval. Nothing but silence — except for an occasional "At'a baby!" from our knowledgeable friend with the country tan; and he seemed to be lauding the cow rather than Francisco.

But to me, neophyte as I was, it was fascinating to observe Francisco's command over the ferocious beast. As he made pass after pass with the cape, each one closer to his own body than the last, the animal came closer too until it seemed that she actually brushed his body as she zoomed past. Finally, bending from his hips, he dragged the cape along the ground. The cow, as if hypnotized, lowered her head until it likewise almost dragged along the ground. Her nose appeared glued to the cape.

Then Francisco performed the circular pass which I believe is known as the *serpentina*. The cow curled around his body in a tight horseshoe.

But the animal was beginning to tire. Her rushes had noticeably slowed. Now her legs buckled and she sank to the ground. Francisco shook the cape before her nose and she struggled up and continued the pursuit. Soon, however, her legs gave way again. This time Francisco laid aside his cape and lowered his head to hers. He glared into her eyes as if daring her to get up and finish him off. But her strength was gone. The fight was over. It was a relief to see Francisco, instead of plunging a sword into her, turn away and in approved bullfighter fashion strut from the ring.

And now occurred another strange phase of this exhibition. Into the ring ran four husky Indian cowboys. As they approached the cow staggered to her feet and in a feeble travesty of defiance lowered her head in fighting pose. The men rushed her, two to her head and two to her rear. The two at the rear seized her tail and distracted her attention while the two at the front each grasped a horn. With all four holding tightly to their respective handles the cow was reduced to practical immobility. Now, with her thus pinioned and subdued, one of the men at the rear released his hold on the tail and drew from some hidden receptacle on his person a shiny object which turned out to be a pair of clippers. Swiftly he clipped, leaving a patch of exposed skin on her side.

"That's her badge of merit," exclaimed our informer. "Now she's entitled to become a mama. She's got what it takes . . . See what I mean when I say de Silva has a practical purpose in staging this fight?"

What followed then was one of the oddest developments of this whole eventful ceremony. The cowboys began escorting the animal from the arena crab fashion — a reluctant crab. With the two men at the tail pulling and the two at the front pushing, they pull-pushed the struggling animal backwards to the gate and out. The why of this peculiar mode of egress is a mystery. I might think it was because the animal had fought so valiantly that the men did not want to subject her to the indignity of turning her back on the ring — I might think so if what happened next had not disillusioned me.

The second heifer lacked the fighting heart. Oh, she made a grandstand entrance all right, and she chased the *banderilleros*, and she tackled the horse. But she soon gave up the fruitless task of trying to toss the horse over the wall. When she backed off and the *picador* pricked her with the spear, instead of plunging back to the attack she flinched and stood still. I thought she showed pretty good judgment. But the *picador* wasn't satisfied. He rammed the spear into her shoulder so brutally that the blood gushed out and ran in a red stream down her shoulder and leg.

The heifer wanted no more of this kind of fighting. She turned and trotted a few steps back out of the spear's reach, and stopped. Her stance was no longer pugnacious. And when she swung her head it was not looking for an object to attack, it was seeking a way out. The four cowboys obliged her. Rushing in they seized her by the same convenient hand-holds they had used on the other cow. Unceremoniously they swung her rear end around so it pointed toward the gate, shifted her into reverse gear, so to speak, and hustled her out.

The bloodshed we had witnessed wasn't much compared to the several bulls that, I understand, ordinarily are killed in the course of a fight. But it was enough. Next to us was a big, husky-looking fellow whose face had turned pasty white. The way he held his fingers to his mouth suggested that his stomach was badly upset.

"My mama didn't raise me to be a bullfighter," he mumbled to me out of the corner of his mouth. "I'm getting out of here."

That, however, was one of those things easier said than done. The stands between us and the stairway were packed solid. To reach it he would have to climb over — *literally* climb over — a long sardine-tight mass of caravaners. But he stood up, looking so determined I suspected that the state of his stomach made his exit mandatory. It looked like one of those unsolvable problems. But the solution was at hand. Two Mexican cowboys whose instantaneous response indicated they had been alerted for just such an emergency, came running across the arena carrying a ladder. They placed the ladder against the wall and motioned our neighbor to climb aboard. Hesitating only a second he followed their instructions. Going that way he had to climb over only two rows of caravaners, and they did their best to move aside and let him through. His wife followed him. I looked at Shirley and she looked at me. Then we both got up and followed our neighbors down the ladder — into the arena. On our way to the nearest escape hatch I brought up the rear, not however without glancing back a couple of times to make sure that no eager beaver jumped the gun and admitted another "bull" ahead of time. I didn't see any animal, but I did see the cowboys racing toward another determined-looking caravaner, with still others standing up and waving.

Outside I once more looked at Shirley. She raised her eyebrows and shrugged, her sign language for "Another experience!"

And what an experience it had turned out to be. But of all the odd quirks of this eventful day, to me the weirdest of all was simply the fact of being there on the hacienda at all. It was like taking a step backward into history. For years I had read of the luxurious life on these vast domains, for the people at the top; a life which rivaled the feudal splendor of the Middle Ages: the-castle-on-the-hill-with-the-peasants'-huts-in-the-valley-below sort of thing. But never had I expected to see it actually being lived. Much, much less had I ever expected to be entertained on one of these princely domains.

As for the bullfight, I'll take football.

CHAPTER VIII

EXPLORING MEXICO ON OUR OWN

Our first trip into Mexico — into the real Mexico, not the border towns — was with the big caravan in 1955. On that trip we traveled about thirty-five hundred miles inside the Mexican borders, approximately half of the distance being with the caravan and half by ourselves. The caravan disbanded in Acapulco, and on the return trip Shirley and I — in contrast to many who organized small groups — elected to go it alone. In 1956 we went back to Mexico alone. In 1957 we joined another caravan but once more took the return trip by ourselves. Since then we have made annual trips into Mexico's hinterland, always by ourselves. My point is this: I don't know that we ever would have got up our courage to go trailering in this foreign land had it not been for the caravan. But once having learned that Mexicans are people like us, only possibly a little more friendly and helpful, we rather enjoy being by ourselves on our explorations.

Now, in this Year of our Lord 1962, after seven years of extremely pleasant associations with Mexico and Mexicans, I want to make this testimony: with no hesitancy whatsoever Shirley and I would enjoy traveling through any and all parts of Mexico by ourselves. In fact we expect to do so. If the old man with the scythe will leave us alone we'll go on indefinitely exploring by trailer other parts of this pleasant land.

We did once have a bad scare. It turned out, however, to be like Bill Nye's troubles: "I've had a lot of troubles in my life but most of them never happened." Our scare was on that trip from Acapulco to El Paso in 1955, our first long Mexican jaunt by ourselves. We thought for sure the Indians were after us. On a long stretch of sparsely settled highway in the late evening when dusk was closing in on us, we were hunting for a place to park overnight. There were no towns in this area, much less any trailer parks. Shirley, studying the map, said: "There's an Indian school marked along here somewhere. If we find it maybe they'll let us park on the campus."

Shortly we came to a set of buildings set back from the road. The structures were large and looked as if they once had been quite imposing. But now they were crumbling, weed-grown, and neglected. Later we learned that they were units of a deserted *hacienda,* one of the great feudal estates that the government had seized and divided the land among the peasants. At the time we thought they were the Indian school buildings, figuring that the school had given up and moved out. We turned in to camp on the deserted campus.

Our arrival disturbed the band of Indians who had moved in and appropriated the buildings, and no doubt were composing themselves for sleep with the coming of darkness. Hearing our car they poured from the buildings and swarmed out to see what was up. Shirley was in the trailer and I was out turning on the bottled gas when I saw them coming. I jumped for the trailer door. Shirley and I held a hurried conference on whether or not to make a break for the car and get out of there. We decided it was too late. Instead we locked the trailer door and closed the curtains. The next few minutes were harrowing. We could hear the Indians' voices at all of the windows and surmised that they were trying to peek in around the edges of the curtains. We sat huddled in our chairs, shivering a little — from the evening chill of course.

By and by, finding that the Indians apparently were not trying to break into the trailer, Shirley mustered her courage and opened a can of soup. While we ate we could hear the Indians talking in low voices a little way from our door. Obviously they were plotting. We did some plotting too. Waiting for the Indians to make their move was too nerve-racking, we'd make a run for the car and *hope* to get away. I threw open the door. The Indians, mostly women and children, were sitting on the ground in a row looking up at the trailer door. When I appeared in the doorway their faces broke into big welcoming grins. I stepped outside. As Shirley followed several of the women held up babies to be admired.

They understood no English and appeared not to understand any of the Spanish phrases I attempted. They jabbered back in Indian talk. Lacking a common language, we got along pretty well. Shirley had some small gifts for the babies, and a good time was had by all.

Another time, a couple of years later, we had another scare. Only this time we were not frightened by Indians, it was by one of those omnipresent individuals, a careless driver. We were traveling light, that is we had left the trailer in a park and were taking a ride through the country. Shirley spoke agitatedly, "There's a truck back of us, following too close."

I glanced back and agreed that it was too close for comfort. My eyes had hardly got back to the road when an emergency arose. An old horse that was feeding beside the road suddenly decided that the grass was greener on the other side and started across in front of us. (Horses, cows, burros, pigs, and various and sundry other animals graze freely along Mexican roadsides; by Mexican law it's the autoist's responsibility to keep from hitting them.) I had to slam on the brakes. Shirley screamed. I glanced back. The truck was careening down on us. Obviously the old vehicle did not have good enough brakes to meet the test. Watching out of the corner of my eye as the ancient truck gyrated back and forth with its tall top-heavy body swaying, I shuddered and waited fearfully for the crash. But at the last possible minute the truck veered off. The driver had chosen to take the ditch instead of hitting us. Fortunately the ditch was shallow. The truck wound up in an adjoining field, right side up. The driver got out, sized up the situation, then turned and waved to us with his thumb and forefinger fixed in the circle that means in Mexico as it does here that everything is okay. He smiled and motioned us to go on.

I've heard tales of Mexican thievery, including the standard joke that Diogenes had to give up searching for an honest man in Mexico because someone stole his lantern. We haven't found it so. Two experiences of ours tend to illustrate the opposite. Both of the examples have to do with stamps — I choose the incidents because of the old wives' tale that Mexican postal employees will steam the stamps off letters and sell them. When we got home from Acapulco I sent a letter to the postmaster with a U.S. dollar bill enclosed, asking him to airmail any mail that had arrived for us after we left. In a few days I got a letter from him with the dollar bill enclosed and the laconic statement, "No mail." Again, during a heavy rainstorm we pulled up in front of a village postoffice and I started to get out in the heavy downpour to post a letter. An elderly man wearing a shabby overcoat stepped up to the auto and courteously asked in broken English if he could be of assistance. Since my letter did not have a stamp on it, I hesitated. Finally I took a chance. I gave the man enough to buy the airmail stamp with a little over, and asked him to do the mailing. As we drove on, Shirley and I, thinking of the steamed-off stamps canard, wondered if we had been silly. Well, probably we were silly to put needless temptation in the way of a man who obviously was poverty-stricken. But when we got home the letter had reached its destination.

Lest it appear that I am trying to build a case that all Mexicans are super-honest, I'll relate an experience tending to show that they are human the same as the rest of us. We were parked temporarily on the outskirts of Tepic. A dapper young officer followed by a rather bedraggled-looking soldier from a nearby military encampment came over to offer assistance. They eagerly accepted our invitation to come in and see the trailer. When I opened the refrigerator disclosing some bottles of beer and invited them to join me, the officer shook his head negatively. Shortly after they left the soldier came back alone. He approached the trailer cautiously from the rear, keeping an eye peeled for the officer. He stepped to the trailer's door and smiled in at me. Then he significantly tipped back his head and held his clenched fist above his mouth with his thumb pointing downward like the neck of a bottle. The gurgling in his throat sounded like "goodgoodgoodgoodgood." I invited him in and he drank the beer *con mucho gusto.*

The only Mexican "bad guy" to give us much concern is a little bug that brings an affliction variously called the Mexican toothache, the Aztec two-step, Montezuma's curse, and the *turista.* All of these names, and the raft of others it receives, are intended to give a humorous tag to a rather common tourist complaint. It is dysentery, and there's nothing humorous about it. Trailer travelers, preparing their own food and taking precautions with drinking water, have little need to fear it. The only time either Shirley or I had even a touch of it was once when we were careless in our choice of a place to eat out.

It has been our fortune to have many kindnesses shown us in Mexico. I am thinking particularly of the many, many times we have asked directions and had the person, instead of giving us oral directions, put himself to considerable trouble to *show us* the way. I am thinking of the time in Morelia when we inquired of a police officer how to find a certain *posada* that had been recommended as a pleasant and "safe" place to get a Mexican meal. The officer indicated that if we wished he would get into our car and show us how to find it. He directed us up a winding road to a picturesque inn in a delightful setting overlooking the city. We made arrangements to bring some guests for dinner the next day, and left. When we got the officer back to his beat — since he had spent a good deal of time with us, and since there seems to be no stigma attached to an officer accepting a gratuity — we offered him some money. He refused it. I resorted to the only surefire method I've found to induce a reluctant Mexican to accept a tip. I asked him if he had children. He held up five fingers, *"Cinco." "Es por los niños"* (it is for the children), I said. Put that way, he accepted the money. Although tipping is widespread throughout Mexico, you'll still find many who are too proud to accept such handouts. It is well to remember that Mexicans are essentially a proud and sensitive people. It takes sensitivity on the part of the tourist to know when to and when not to tip. Much depends upon the spirit and attitude of the giver, for "the gift without the giver is bare."

I am thinking of the Saturday night we parked for an overnight stop at the outskirts of a village whose name I have forgotten. At dark the lights came on, but as is not uncommon in small Mexican towns they soon flickered out. And stayed out. But that did not interfere with the planned Saturday night activities. On schedule the band struck up a tune. Soon groups of people, talking and laughing, began passing the trailer on their way to the village square. One couple stopped and in halting English asked us to go with them to hear "boogy-woogy." We went, and in most pleasant company, with the public square dimly lighted with lanterns, listened to a program of hauntingly sweet Mexican music and American "boogy-woogy."

I am happy to report that not all the kindnesses we have witnessed have been by the Mexicans. We've seen numerous instances where the milk of human kindness has flowed in the other direction. One example we uncovered in Guadalajara. Looking up some former Los Angeles neighbors, a retired army colonel and his wife who have been making their home in Mexico for the last several years, we found something that touched our hearts. In the colonel's home, living with them as part of the family, were two teenage Mexican girls and their old grandmother. This arrangement started when the colonel engaged the older of the girls to do housework. Being childless, not from choice, they soon became attached to the quiet, efficient, attractive girl. Before long they were sending her to school, dressing and caring for her as if she were their own child. When the girl timidly made it known that she had a younger sister who would have to go out to work since the family had insufficient means to feed their large and growing numbers, the colonel drove to the family's little mud shack in the country and brought the young girl — really just a child — home with him. Later the grandmother joined the group to help care for the girls. When we returned to the States we corresponded with the colonel. His letters were filled with the joys they were having from the girls. An extract from one of the letters will illustrate:

> . . . This year on our annual visit to California, Elvira, our eldest, will come with us. She will have finished her course in beauty culture, and as she has worked like one possessed on her English, which was our only requirement for the trip, she more than deserves to go. We are looking forward to showing her a new world; going by way of San Diego to show her her first zoo. Don't you rather envy us?
>
> Silvina, our younger girl, has entered the American School this year. She is now thirteen and has become a very pretty, unselfish, lovable child. Our problem with her, as with Elvira, is to keep her from studying too much. Their grandmother, whom we call *Mamacita*, watches over us as well as the girls, treating us as if we were her own children . . .
>
> So you see our Mexican family has become very much a part of us . . .
>
> *Postscript. A year later:* Elvira is now out of the nest and self-supporting. We have taken in a third child from the same family to live with us . . .

In a larger sense (to use Lincoln's phraseology) our country as a whole is extending the friendly hand across the border through our support of such organizations and programs as The Good Neighbor Policy, The Alliance for Progress, and Unesco. At Lake Patzcuaro we were privileged to observe the activities of one of these groups.

On the palatial estate of the former President Lazaro Cardenas, presented by President Cardenas for the purpose, we witnessed the activities of CREFAL (*Centro Regional de Educacion Fundamental Para la America Latina* — a branch of Unesco). Here selected students from all of the Latin American States are permitted to come and study how to teach their own people a better way of life. Through the use of brightly colored posters the school was demonstrating such simple phases of civilized living as the following: how to build sanitary outhouses to aid in keeping flies from flying directly from the privy to the family table, how to build a simple stove and chimney so that the housewife would not have to cook at a stick fire on the floor of a smoke-choked room, how to prevent cats and other animals from falling into the family well. It was grass-roots education taught in a manner understandable by the most untutored. One outgrowth of such teaching was reported in the April 1962 *Reader's Digest* under the title "The Golden Eggs of Patzcuaro." It gives vivid testimony to the worth of such teachings — in this case among the Tarascan Indians of the Lake Patzcuaro region.

Mexico is changing. It is fascinating to sit in on the emergence of a rapidly developing nation. During the brief years that we have known Mexico we have witnessed many examples of striking change. Not all of the changes, to be sure, have been good. Many merchants are becoming tourist-wise and tourist-hardened. Prices are climbing. To tourists the rising prices are an inconvenience, even an annoyance; but you still can live cheaper in Mexico than at home. To many Mexicans the rising price scale is stark tragedy.

But on the whole the changes are for the better. First and foremost, from the viewpoint of a trailerist, is the amazing improvement in trailer parks. New modern parks are springing up at an unbelievable rate. Also the roads are improving. One can travel up and down the country and back and forth across it, that is on main roads, without getting off pavement — except for minor detours. In most of the large cities and in some of the smaller ones, *supermercados*, selling groceries after the fashion of our supermarkets, are replacing the old grocery cubbyholes. Guadalajara has an enormous new public market that architecturally would be a credit to any city anywhere in the world. Mexico City has a university with buildings almost unexcelled in beauty and set on a campus of the greatest charm. Near the cities of Obregon, Navajoa, and Los Mochis is a huge irrigation project that has brought water to thousands of thirsty acres and caused them to burst forth with crops that might well make any other country jealous. But probably of greatest significance, in the long run, is the change in education, particularly in public school education for the masses. Shirley and I had a dramatic demonstration of this change in the open country near San Blas.

I had stopped to take a color picture of an especially lovely

Bougainvillea vine climbing over the thatched roof of a mud cottage. Shirley called my attention to an odd mumbling sound coming from a mud hut on the other side of the road. Upon investigation we found it to be a country school, with the children studying aloud. I had not known that this custom still obtained anywhere on our continent. Our curiosity had drawn us close to the hut's open door — providing the only light in the room, there was no window. The teacher, a personable young man, in perfect English invited us in to visit the school. When we stepped in upon the bare dirt floor, swept scrupulously clean, the children courteously rose to greet us and stood politely facing us until I motioned for them to sit down. We noticed that most of the youngsters had pronounced Indian features. We stayed long enough to see some of the children's work, and were pleased at what we saw. Two years later when we passed through this area we naturally were on the lookout for the school. We found it, but it was no longer a school. It was occupied by a family, with the customary pigs and chickens as well as children running in and out of the open door. A mile or so up the road we found a new school, clean, neat, and brightly painted. There were many windows. The yard was surrounded by a fence behind which the children were playing a recess game. The contrast was symbolical of what is taking place in Mexico.

An article in the *National Geographic* for October 1961 reports that since 1940 Mexico's population has doubled, now reaching 35 million. During this period its exports have tripled. Its electric power output has quadrupled. Its steel production has multiplied seven times.

In spite of the changes taking place, there is still enough of the old and settled to charm those who prefer the old Mexico. Mexico is often called the land of contrasts. In no respect is this contrast more striking than in the close juxtaposition of the old and the new. A few examples: In Granajuato we saw a display of the most modern, up-to-date farm machinery; within a dozen miles we saw a man plowing a field with oxen and a crooked-stick plow. On the highway we meet buses as modern as tomorrow; we also meet many men riding little burros as did Abraham, Isaac, and Jacob. In a city where luxurious hotels care for the most affluent, we saw an inn with stalls for the travelers' burros, reminding one of a certain inn of Bethlehem twenty centuries ago. In cities and towns where public water runs through pipes and out of faucets, one sees men passing with yokes over their shoulders balancing great oil drums of water from a public well. Once while riding on a public bus we met a large group of men, women, and children with banners announcing that it was such and such a village on a pilgrimage to a holy shrine — like the Crusades.

An Indian woman was sitting on a curb, holding her baby. She smiled when I showed interest in the child. But when I indicated that I would like to take the baby's picture, in obvious fear she hastily covered the baby's face and frowningly said, "No! No!" Similarly, I saw three men crossing a river standing in a boat and poling the boat over swift water. Thinking the scene picturesque I stepped to the car to get my camera. When I looked again the men had vanished. I realized what was wrong. I had forgotten the superstition that when you take a person's picture you do damage to his soul. The boat was drifting downstream. When it touched shore, the men scrambled up from the floor of the boat and hastily disappeared into the bushes.

In the *Barranca de Cobre*, a canyon deeper than the Colorado River Canyon, I am told that there are still Indians who catch their game by running it down and strangling it. I know from personal observation that many Indians throughout Mexico get their fish by casting butterfly nets for them. No, those old Mexican customs haven't all disappeared yet.

Mexico, the land of contrasts. The land of the *fiesta* and the *siesta*, of gay celebration and easy relaxation. The land of hard work and satisfying rest. The land of color, of music, of flowers. The land of extreme poverty but also great happiness. The land of warm smiles and helpfulness. An easy land to love. A friendly people hard not to love.

If you would like to visit Mexico but are, as we were, somewhat timid about it, one good way to break the ice is to do what we did, join a trailer caravan. If that doesn't appeal, there are other helps, a few of which are listed below:

1. Someone has said, "If you're going to have a flat tire, Mexico is a good place to have it." He was referring to the Mexican Government's "Green Fleet," a fleet of cars that tour the highways looking for trouble — trouble that they can alleviate. Minor vehicle repairs, emergency gasoline and oil, tire changes, information; all of these services are yours free. Write to *Mexican Government Tourism Department, Paseo de la Reforma 35, Mexico City* for a free pamphlet that gives all the information.

2. Another free pamphlet put out by the *Mexican Government Tourism Department*, labeled simply *Dear Friend*, will give you advice on altitude, rainfall and climate conditions, travel wardrobe, medical care, requirements for entry, Mexican money, accommodations and restaurants, and numerous other subjects.

3. A free brochure, *Mexican Adventure by Travel Trailer*, giving advice on roads, trailer parks, insurance, what to do and see, etc., may be obtained from *Mobile Homes Manufacturing Association, 20 Wacker Dr., Chicago 6, Illinois*.

If these publications do not answer your questions, write an open letter to the communications columns of any of the trailer magazines.

I shall be surprised if you do not get a perfect flood of replies from enthusiastic trailerists to Mexico.

Adios. Hasta luego. See you soon — in Mexico.

CHAPTER IX

UPHILL-FLOWING RIVERS AND SKY-HIGH FISHING

As our 1959 trailer caravan to Eastern Canada, consisting of more than two hundred trailers, neared Ottawa I pulled off the highway and into a country gasoline station. Close to the pumps was a combined store and house occupied by the proprietor of the gasoline station. On the steps of the house sat a little four- or five-year-old girl, her eyes bulging with the wonder of watching the long, long line of trailers slipping past.

Shirley leaned out of the car window and smilingly said hello to the little girl.

Instead of replying the little girl asked, "Have you got a doggie?"

I wondered what had put that thought into the child's mind, until I remembered that in the car that had pulled out of the station just as we pulled in, the woman passenger in the car had held two fluffy poodles in her arms.

"No," said Shirley, "no doggie."

After a minute's silence the child popped another question. "Where do you live?"

"In California," replied Shirley.

"That way?" asked the child, pointing the way we were headed.

"No, *that* way," said Shirley, pointing back.

"And do you ever *stay* there?" asked the child.

Shirley explained that sometimes we stayed there but that at present we were living in the little house-on-wheels hooked on behind our car.

And so we were. A unique feature of these trailer caravans is that all of us in the caravan actually set up housekeeping in our own little homes in various parts of the foreign countries we travel in. The full significance of this fact seemed to burst full bloom upon a new caravaner who parked next to us in Ottawa.

"Well," said he as he finished erecting the canvas awning over his trailer doorway and eased himself into his comfortable folding canvas chair, "I'm living in the Capital of Canada."

Besides Ottawa we lived a few days each in Montreal, Quebec, and numerous other cities of Canada. Also we lived in various provincial parks. And we lived in numerous towns and villages throughout the provinces of Ontario, Quebec (including the Gaspé Peninsula), New Brunswick, Nova Scotia, and Prince Edward Island.

Just to mention a few of the experiences of this caravan will illustrate the types of adventures we enjoyed: a tour through the "Soo" Locks at Sault Ste. Marie, the busiest locks on earth (according to a brochure distributed at the locks), carrying more tonnage than the combined tonnage of the Panama and Suez canals; being honored guests of Canada's capital city and setting up housekeeping in one of its handsomest city parks; bivouacked beside the famous St. Lawrence Seaway where we could take our chairs and sit on the bank watching huge ocean-going ships ply their way to and from Detroit, Chicago, Duluth, and all the other Great Lakes cities; getting acquainted with picturesque Quebec City; viewing the charming little fishing villages and the rugged shore line of the Gaspé peninsula; buying bread and rolls baked by farm wives in outdoor ovens; visiting in Halifax the oldest protestant church in Canada, St. Paul's, and St. Paul's "baby," the "Little Dutch Church" nearby (and seeing in the Little Dutch churchyard the grave of Restella Jane Ratsy, the only member of the British royal family buried outside of the British Isles); breathing the sentiment-laden air of Nova Scotia's "Acadia" country, immortalized in Longfellow's *Evangeline*. All this and more, much more.

To say nothing of rivers that run uphill.

The whole caravan saw these rivers that run backwards. Such phenomena are common throughout much of the route that the caravan took. They are called "Tidal Bores."

In case you do not live near the ocean and are therefore unfamiliar with this ocean terminology, it means simply that the tide comes in so big and so fast and so powerful that, you might say, it pushes the river back on its heels and makes it turn around and run the other way.

On the shores of the Bay of Fundy — that enormous body of sea water bounded on two sides by Nova Scotia, on the third side by New Brunswick and our state of Maine, and on the fourth side by the Atlantic Ocean — the towns and cities which are situated at rivers' mouths consider tidal bores to be an important stock in trade. The chambers of commerce use them as tourist attractions. The accepted practice is for a town to erect a sign giving their tidal bore's time-table — and perhaps proclaiming to the world that their tidal bore is bigger and better than that of other towns. The timetable, which is changed daily according to the changing tides, gives the exact minute the next bore is due to come in and do its stuff with the river. And so well disciplined are the bores that they perform pretty much on schedule.

At Truro, Nova Scotia (in the very heart of Acadia), Shirley and I drove a mile and a half out of town to watch our first tidal bore, in the Salmon River. Having read in the local paper when the bore would arrive, and knowing from infancy that time and tide wait for no man, we arrived well ahead of time. There, in company with many other camera-laden tourists, we waited impatiently, vaguely wondering if maybe just this once the phenomenon might fail to occur. Certainly there was nothing in the appearance of the innocent-looking river to suggest a major upheaval about to take place.

Then suddenly someone called out, "There she comes!"

We looked off toward the bay and there coming around a bend in the river was a wave stretching clear across the river and headed our way. We watched the wave of brown, frothy water come past us and move majestically upstream. Following the wave was a great flock of sea birds feasting upon the "sea food" washed in by the tide.

In a matter of minutes the Salmon River, which up till then had been placidly flowing its wonted course down to the sea, had turned tail and was running the other way. Not only that, but all the sandbars and shallow places began to disappear. Shortly the moderately shallow, smooth-flowing, ocean-bound stream became a deep, forbidding-looking, wrong-way-Corrigan, uphill-flowing mighty river.

It is only fair to say that, in the face of all the buildup, that initial view of a tidal bore was a bit dissappointing. That first broad wave that came in from the ocean was rather low, not very impressive. In fact, from our position high on the bank it didn't appear to be much bigger than the wave sent out by a big motor boat. Later we learned that it is only when there is a storm at sea that the initial incoming wave makes a spectacular appearance. Then, driven by hurricane-like winds, it rushes in as a surging wall of water many feet high.

But always, in stormy weather or in calm weather, the flood that *follows* that first wave is an eye-widening sight. And no wonder the follow-up flood is impressive; it has the whole tidal power of the Atlantic Ocean back of it. And a fearsome sight indeed is that deep, dark, irresistible tide forcing the river back uphill.

Just why the tidal bores of the Bay of Fundy are so much bigger than elsewhere is not easy to understand. Not for the layman, anyhow. But at Moncton, New Brunswick, the Chamber of Commerce presents not only the bore's timetable, it also attempts to give some aid to understanding the nature of the bore.

The sign says:

> No one really knows what causes the famous Tidal Bore. It is assumed that the funnel-like shape of the Bay of Fundy makes for the swift rise of the ocean tides which wash up-river for over twenty miles.
>
> Tides normally rise slowly, taking several hours to reach the flood.
>
> At Moncton the tide comes all at once. In a few hours after the Bore has passed the broad river basin is filled with thirty feet of water . . .

So, even though only partly understood, backward-running rivers became a familiar sight to the caravaners.

As for fish hanging tree-high like fruit waiting to be picked, most of the caravan did not see that. Well, for that matter, neither did Shirley and I. But we almost did, and thereby hangs a tale.

There came a day when Shirley and I felt an overwhelming compulsion to get away by ourselves and explore more of this exciting country on our own. Yielding to the compulsion we left the caravan. A few days later, while traveling leisurely on the Nova Scotia road that runs along the north shore of Minas Basin, we stopped for lunch in a school yard. The school being situated on an eminence where the view was pleasing, after we ate we stood outside the trailer enjoying the scenery. Since it was summer, school was not in session and there was no one to bother us. In an unhurried mood, we took plenty of time for viewing and for letting the peaceful countryside minister to our souls.

We fell to dreaming of Evangeline, for this was still in the midst of Acadia. Directly south of us, across the Basin, lay the town of Grand Pré. We tried to locate it, but the distance was too great; we could not see it. Longfellow was at his best in recounting the pathetic story of frustrated love between Evangeline and Gabriel. The opening lines of the epic poem have always clung hauntingly to my memory. Unwittingly I started to speak them aloud.

This is the forest primeval.
The murmuring pines and the hemlocks stand,
Like druids of eld . . .

My recitation was interrupted by the sound of a vehicle on the highway. Few vehicles of any kind had we encountered since leaving the caravan. And this one was not a speeding automobile. It was a team of horses hitched to a wagon. The driver was a farmer of the neighborhood, dressed in his working clothes. "Whoa," he said to the horses, and then slouched comfortably in the wagon seat he prepared for a sociable chat.

"Enjoyin' the scenery?"

"We certainly are," said we enthusiastically.

"See you have a Californy license. What part you hail from?"

"Winters we live in the desert near Palm Springs. Summers we . . ." I gestured toward the trailer.

"Palm Springs, eh? Don't know as I ever heerd of that place . . . But say, have you ever heerd of the kind of fishing they call sky fishing?"

"Sky fishing?" I said. "Can't say I ever did."

"Sometimes," he said, with an odd little twist to the lines around his mouth, "they call it horse-and-wagon fishing."

"Can't say's I ever heard of that either," I admitted. "Where . . . ?"

"Y'ought to see it whilst you're in these parts. Giddap, Ned, Maud."

And he pulled away, leaving us with our curiosity all aquiver —

as he had intended. There being no one else in sight we had no way to satisfy our curiosity until we came to a country store a few miles up the road. After we had bought some supplies I asked the proprietor.

"You know anything about this sky-high, horse-and-wagon fishing?"

"Sure do," said he, lifting the glass cover from a large cheese and cutting a shaving which he nibbled as he talked. "Have some?" And he whittled a shaving for each of us.

After sampling the cheese, expressing our approval and buying a pound, I asked, "Anything to it? Worth looking into, I mean?"

"Sure is," said he emphatically. "Doggondest fishing you ever laid eyes on. Don't miss it."

"Where do they do it?"

"T'aint exactly a *they*. It's a *he*. Only one man, 's'far's I know, ever does it. Russell Mack ... Which way you headed?"

"Toward Parrsboro, and on west."

"H'mm, y'u should've turned off way back there, just beyond that school house you passed."

We knew the school house he meant. It was the one where we had lunched, and had our curiosity excited by the laconic farmer.

"Tell you what you do," the groceryman continued, "you go back t'other side of the school house, to the first corner, and take the road headed south. Follow that to River Hebert — that's a town. Beyond Hebert you'll have seven miles of dirt road 'fore you get to Minude — that's where Russell lives and does his fishing ... Road's not too good. But they've been working on it lately. May be all right by now."

To backtrack needlessly is not a pleasant prospect. Neither is a dirt road. But caravaners learn to take the bad with the good. And, actually, when you are on a ten-thousand-mile vacation jaunt, as Shirley and I were, a few miles more or less do not matter much. And if this aerial fishing was what it was cracked up to be, we ought to see it. So back we went.

But we found that the seven miles of dirt road in question did matter much. Very much indeed. Positively and unequivocally, they were the worst seven miles we have encountered in our travels east, west, north, and south. They were simply awful. The road crew, which consisted of neighborhood farmers armed with horse-powered plows and scrapers, had not finished their work. In fact, they were slap dab in the middle of their work. I think we struck the spot at the worst possible time. What they had done so far was to scrape the turf and boulders along with great quantities of pulverized dirt — the driest, dustiest, most penetrating dirt these old eyes have ever smarted from — from the edges of the road and piled the entire mess up in the middle of the roadbed.

Nobody made any effort to stop us. The road crew stood to one side and let us barge into the upheaval. And once in, it seemed best to forge ahead. We had no idea that the carnage would last the entire seven miles. But it did. And we emerged from the ordeal with the car and trailer filled with the powder-fine dust, and ourselves choking. As I say, it was the worst piece of road we have encountered, and we have encountered some dillies.

After the seven miles of "improved" road, when we were traveling again on just ordinarily bad dirt road, we came upon a man who was scything weeds at the side of the road.

"We on the right road to Minude?" I asked.

"Yep," he said, pausing in his work and leaning on his scythe.

"About how far is it?"

"Well," said he, "you're practically there now."

I glanced around but could see nothing indicating a town.

"Who you lookin' for?"

"Russell Mack. You know him?"

"Yep. Figured that was who you wanted ... See that house over yonder?" He pointed to a weather-beaten farmhouse a few rods up the road.

I thanked him and prepared to start on, when he spoke again. His remark brought us up short.

"Mack don't do that kind of fishin' no more."

"He what!" I exclaimed.

"Nope. No more ... But you'd best go on and talk to Mrs. Mack — don't think Mack is home today; he's working somewheres — she c'n tell you more about it than I can."

Mrs. Mack, a slender, pleasant-faced woman surrounded by several children two of whom clung to her skirts, confirmed what we had been told, that Mr. Mack was working, and that he had discontinued, temporarily at least, his unique type of fishing.

"Had to give it up," she said. "But come on in. I'll show you some pictures."

She showed us pictures, meanwhile giving a running commentary of how the fishing was done.

"The little bay back of our house is dry as a bone when the tide is out," she said. "Well, Mack got the idea of setting up a row of nets, a whole string of them, staking them down to the bare ground. See, this picture shows how it looks with the tide out, and Mack out there with his horses and wagon setting up his nets on the dry ground. When the tide comes in it brings in fish, sometimes lots of them. Then when the tide goes back out again, it leaves the fish hanging in the nets. See, this here picture shows how they look when they're hanging in the nets. That's Mack and his hired man out there with the team and wagon. They shake the net and the fish fall off; all they have to do is pick 'em up ... except sometimes when a fish gets stuck in the net by his gills, then they have to climb the ladder and pull him loose."

"Well," I said, "someone told us Mr. Mack did the oddest kind of fishing anybody ever laid eyes on, and I believe it."

"Folks come a long ways to see it."

"Anybody from as far as California?" I inquired.

"No. Guess you're the fust ones. But from most every place else, seems like."

"Why did he give it up?"

"Had to. Got too tough."

"Tough?"

"Yes, dogfish. Got so they come in with every tide. Riddled the fish in the nets. Riddled the nets too, for that matter. They ate up all the profits."

Dogfish, I learned later, are a variety of small shark.

"Do you suppose," I inquired, "after Mr. Mack has laid off for a while the dogfish will stop coming in and he can start fishing again?"

"Couldn't say," said Mrs. Mack. "But tell you what, if you'd like to see some real good pictures, better than these here ones, you go and see the editor of the paper in Amherst. He took a lot of pictures and wrote quite a piece about Mack's fishing."

Following her advice, I got acquainted with Editor Andres of the *Amherst Daily News*. He appeared surprised and disappointed to learn of Mr. Mack's quitting.

"If he's quit, for good, that's the last of the horse-and-wagon fishing. I hope not. It's something entirely unique."

And I hope not too. Sometime I'd like to go back again — yes, even over the dirt road — to see if the horse-and-wagon sky-fishing has ever been resumed. But meanwhile, through the generosity of Mr. Andres, here are pictures of the kind of fishing Shirley and I almost saw.

CHAPTER X

TRAILERING TROUBLES

"These birds that write for trailer magazines," said the man loudly, "tell all the good points about trailering and none of the bad."

The fellow was leafing through the trailer magazines on the table in our Palm Springs trailer supply store. I had gone in to buy a new piece of sewer hose, which by the way I carry in a metal tube under the trailer. Since the store was busy several of us were waiting to be served. Glancing around to see that everybody was paying attention, the noisy fellow grumbled on, "Reading these things," he thumped the table for emphasis, "you'd think that everything was always just hunky-dory, no troubles at all . . ." And so on.

I'm one of the "birds" who sometimes write for trailer magazines. But I'm the kind of "bird" who, in a situation like this, think up my good answer after the time to use it has gone by. So I didn't say anything. But now that I've had time to think up my answer, if I had the fellow here beside me I'd say:

"Look here, you . . ."

But come to think of it he was pretty big and husky. Maybe I'd leave off the "you." I'd say:

"Look here, nobody *makes* us write those articles. And I know from experience that those magazines don't pay enough to make a man sell his integrity. We simply call 'em as we see 'em."

Then, if he was still listening, I'd go on. "For that matter, nobody *makes* us go on trailering. We keep on doing it because we love it." Then I'd take a dig at the fellow. I'd say, "Anybody make *you* go on trailering? Or reading trailer magazines?"

Then, after I'd given him a good talking to like that, I'd make him feel good by admitting all that he had said. I'd agree that we writers no doubt do tend to play up the pleasant aspects of trailering and play down the unpleasant. It's only fair to recognize, I'd tell him, that trailering troubles do arise, usually small ones but sometimes big ones.

Therefore, for the sake of our loud-talking friend, and as a fair warning to anyone who might conceivably plan to begin trailer touring because of reading these pages, here goes for a peek at some trailering troubles.

Troubles, as everyone knows, come like bananas, in bunches. You may go along for months, even years, with everything functioning like a well-oiled machine, then blooie! Everything seems to go wrong at once.

That's the way it happened to us one year on our way down from Washington. On that one trip we had more trials and tribulations than on a half-dozen other trips. It wasn't typical, but — well, it will give a prospective trailerist a picture of the sort of things that may happen.

"Did you hear it rain in the night?" asked Shirley as I rolled out of bed on the morning we were to start home.

"No," I replied, "I slept too soundly. Sorry."

And I *was* sorry. I enjoy hearing the drumming of rain on our aluminum roof. But then the full impact of her words penetrated my sleepy head, and I yipped, "Rain!"

"Yes, rain," she said accusingly, as if I was to blame for the rain.

I knew what she was fussing about. The night before she had tried to get me to hook up the trailer and move it off the grass and onto the more solidly-packed-and-turfed woods trail. "Suppose it should rain in the night," she said. "Your clover lawn will make a beautiful slippery-slide."

"Take a look at the sky," I said. "You're always imagining something is going to happen. Besides," I added, "you know if we move onto the trail we can't have electricity, and we can't use our bathroom. We'd better stay right here till morning."

"All right," she said. "But don't forget if ... "

Now she displayed her sterling character by refraining from uttering the logical I-told-you-so's. She just *looked* them.

I got the car hitched to the trailer without too much trouble, started the motor and slowly eased into automatic shift. Before I knew it, the wheels were spinning and had dug themselves a couple of inches down into the nice soft clover. I got out and put brush under the wheels and tried again. They sank a little deeper.

"Here, try this," said Shirley, handing me the welcome mat. The wheel threw it twenty feet out behind and sank another inch into the clover. I let air out of the tires, as much as I dared with nine miles of driving ahead of us before we could get more air. The wheels widened their trenches and sank in another inch. By now the rubber was smoking and smelling like a new tar roof.

Finally I disconnected the car and drove to a farmer neighbor's. He came over with his tractor and pulled us out. "Forget it," he said when I tried to pay him. Thus we had another occasion for thanking the Lord for good neighbors.

The next day, over in Montana (we were taking a round-about route home) we had a puncture. With the perverse luck that accompanied us on this trip, the tire naturally went flat far out in the open country. I drew to the side of the road and disconnected the car from the trailer. But when I started to jack up the car, I found that the road's sloping shoulder posed a problem. The car began slowly to shift ditchward. Before taking the final plunge, however, it trembled, hesitated, and stopped. I tiptoed out of the way and stood holding my breath.

"There's a farmhouse over there," said Shirley. "Shall I go see if they have a telephone?"

"Please do," I replied, without taking my eyes from the jack and using as little breath as possible, "but move softly."

It developed that the farmer didn't have a telephone, but he brought Shirley back in his truck. He looked over the situation, removed his cap and scratched his head, and looked again. Then he got a jack and some blocks of wood from his truck, braced the jack on the blocks, hoisted the car; and went right ahead and put on my spare. I couldn't force any money on him. Again, thank the Lord for good farm neighbors, especially neighbors whom you've never seen before and may never see again, but who have the good-neighbor spirit.

In the middle of the morning while we were getting filled with gas, the attendant asked, "You headed east?"

"Yes," I said, "as far as Butte. But we're following the birds. We're headed for California."

"You didn't get started after the birds soon enough," he said "Look there:"

In the distance ahead we could see black clouds. And they meant business. In the vicinity of Butte we encountered the season's first snowfall. It was September fifteenth.

Perhaps a word of explanation is due as to why we were in Montana on our way from Washington to California. The reason was some rheumatic pains Shirley had developed in her back and shoulders. Various trailer friends had recommended the hot mineral baths at Lava Hot Springs, Idaho, for such conditions, stating that there was a pleasant trailer park there to accommodate bathers. We were going to California by way of Montana, Idaho, Utah, and Nevada, with the plan of stopping off in Idaho for some hot baths.

The storm turned into a yowling Montana blizzard. In the midst of it, while we were on a twisting mountain road with the visibility near zero, out of the corner of my left eye I saw movement. I glanced that way to see a truck passing. The truck's headlights were on. So were ours. But at that minute a car burst out of the snow screen ahead, coming toward us. Its headlights were not on. If they had been, perhaps we could have seen it sooner. As it was, the car must have been not more than two hundred feet away when it materialized out of the snowy whiteness. The driver evidently slammed on his brakes, for the car began to slue back and forth across the highway. The truck's airbrakes made their loud *psst, psst,* and its tires began to screech on the pavement . . . Well, we all got safely by. It was just another of those near misses. Afterward Shirley and I pulled to the side of the road and let our nerves settle back into their normal channels.

This experience prompts me to make a general comment about road hazards in trailering. It is my considered opinion that you're less likely to have accidents with a trailer than without one. Speed is the great accident-causer, the great killer. And with a trailer, half the pressure for speed is eliminated. You don't have to get any particular place by mealtime, or by nightfall. Your trailer takes care of that. I know for a fact that since we've started trailering we drive slower, and we come in more rested at night. As for slowing up other traffic, maybe a little slowing up isn't too bad. And furthermore, we're not as slow as big trucks are going *up*hill, And, praise be to Allah, we're a whole lot slower going *down*hill. However, there's no gainsaying the fact that there's always an element of danger on any highway, with or without a trailer, the worst danger being that of a loose nut *behind* the wheel.

The prospective trailerist, however, should know that he, too, has a responsibility. Common human decency, as well as regard for the traffic laws, should prompt him to keep well to the right side of the road so that faster traffic may safely pass. He should likewise, when on an uphill pull, seek opportunities to pull aside and let other cars by. Experienced trailerists have learned to observe these courtesies — partly as a measure of self-preservation.

I suppose it is tempting fate to brag — or is it bragging when you tell the truth? In the fifteen years that we have been trailering (seven years before we retired, and now eight years of retirement), we have yet to get the first bump or scratch on car or trailer from contact with any other vehicle when we have been pulling a trailer.

When we got to the hot springs that day the snow was still falling and the air was cold.

"Br-r-r-r," said Shirley, "I don't want a bath. Keep right on going."

The next day, farther south, the storm changed its complexion. The snow stopped, but black clouds hung overhead ominously. By mid-afternoon the sky looked so threatening that we decided to call it a day. We pulled into a little village and inquired for a trailer park. There was none. We stopped at the office of a grist mill and asked the proprietor if he minded if we parked in the vacant lot next door (a graveled lot; no danger of sticking in mud), so we could get off the street.

"Sure thing," he said, "pull right in here next the building; it'll give you some protection . . . or say, better yet, pull over there a bit and back 'er right in betwixt the mill and that old shed. That way you'll get protection from both sides . . . Here, I'll help you park."

Then came his inexpert assistance. I started to back into the narrow slot between the building and the shed, craning my neck around trying to see the end of the trailer. But I couldn't see it well enough to be sure just which way the trailer was headed. I had to depend on my "assistant."

"You're coming about right," he said. "Keep coming just the way you are."

The man was waving me back, a satisfied grin on his face. He was obviously enjoying being helpful. I continued to back, slowly.

"Easy now ... slow ... steady," he cautioned. Then his voice suddenly took on a frantic note. "Whoa!"

I stopped.

"Cut 'er the other way!" he commanded.

"Which way?" I inquired, thinking I had been backing straight.

"Why, t'other way from what you're going." He didn't add the word Stupid, but his voice indicated it. "Pull your wheel to the right," he finally said, and as I complied, "Tha--t--'s i--t, steady now ... take it easy ... Aw! you twisted it *too far* to the right. Pull up there ahead and try it again, an' this time don't twist the wheel so far ... "

I tried again, backing slowly and carefully.

"That's it! ... Keep right on that way ... Fine, fine ... Hold it! HOLD IT! Aw, you've come too far this way ... Pull 'er up again ... and cut 'er the other way ... "

I'm actually a little proud of my trailer backing. There's not a great deal to it once you get the hang of it, remembering always to turn your wheel exactly opposite from what you'd do if you didn't have a trailer on. (A bit of advice at this point for new trailerists: get out in an open field or a vacant parking lot and practice a little before you take to the highway. The knack will soon come to you.) But I knew that something had to be done in this situation. You can't make much headway with a "Cut-'er-the-other-way!" adviser.

I got out of the car and pretended to look over the situation, taking lots of time. Then, with my most ingratiating smile, I said, "Tell you, my wife and I've worked out a kind of system. Let's get her over here. She may be able to help."

With that Shirley, who had modestly kept in the background, stepped over and I climbed behind the wheel. Shirley took a position back of the car where I could see her without putting a crick in my neck. She sized up the situation and motioned with one hand for me to turn the end of the trailer just slightly toward her. I knew which way to turn my driving wheel to accomplish that, and did so. She motioned me to come on back. I did that, slowly. She motioned me to keep on coming, and I did so. After a bit she motioned for the end of the trailer to head slightly in the other direction, and I turned the wheel accordingly. After a bit she held up both hands, indicating that I should come about a yard farther. I did so. Then she held the flat of her hand toward me, indicating that was far enough. I stopped, and got out of the car.

"I'll be damned!" said the man with a grin, his affable nature once more in the saddle. "Well, make yourselves comfortable ... There's a wash room next to the side door. I'll leave it unlocked if you like, provided you'll see that it's locked again in the morning if you leave before I get here."

During the night we had a rip-snorter of a storm. Lightning, thunder, and rain barraged us. The rain pounding on our roof went far beyond the "merry tune" stage. It roared. The thunder reverberated fearsomely through the narrow canyon between the buildings, and seemed to shake our trailer with its wild power. The lightning, when it flashed, lit up the inside of the trailer and everything around us. I felt grateful for the rubber insulation of the tires between us and the ground.

The next morning the bright, clear, clean world compensated in large measure for the inconvenience — and, I confess it, the uneasiness — of the night before.

When we got out of the mountains the weather began to warm up. So did our spirits. As we approached Las Vegas I said to Shirley, "What do you say we see the bright lights tonight? Sort of an antidote for all our troubles of the trip."

"Suits me," she said. "Let's do it."

"Big dinner in some swell joint," I went on, warming to my subject, "girl show, gambling, the works. One wild night."

"We-l-l..." said Shirley.

But my mind was made up. We were really going to see the town.

As a starter for our big night we hunted up the most expensive-looking trailer park we could find. It was located near the center of activities, had tall shade trees and blooming flowers, and a general air of luxury. It charged as much as we have ever paid for a night's parking, $2.50. The customary charge, through the years, has crept up from $1 to $1.50, $1.75, and occasionally on to $2.00 tops. But this was luxurious Las Vegas and we didn't object to the $2.50.

The proprietress of the park, taking it for granted that we were going to see the sights, offered advice on how we could get the most for our money.

"I'll tell you right where to go," she said. "You not only get the best dinner for your money, but there's also a free floor show with the dinner."

That sounded good, so we took her advice. But when we arrived at the restaurant about seven o'clock the place was crowded. We edged in and worked our way between the gambling machines and through the crowd, heading toward what we thought was the dining room. We were pleased to note that there were but few people lined up ahead of us. Evidently most of the people were there for gambling and not for eating. Or so we thought, for a while. But when we got near the head of our line we found that all we were going to get here was tickets. The dining room entrance was around a corner, in another alcove. There was a throng around the door.

Our tickets were numbered 163 and 164. Just as we joined this line, the ticket-taker announced, "Numbers 74 and 75!" And two people at the head of the line were admitted to the dining room.

I worked my way back to the ticket dispenser. "Any idea how long we'll have to wait?" I asked him, holding up my tickets.

"Oh, quite a while," he added, "Circulate around. Have some fun. You'll have plenty of time."

So we circulated. But watching other people gamble soon grows tiresome. I turned to Shirley.

"Why don't you try your luck?"

"I believe I shall," she said, daringly.

So she had a fifty cent piece changed into dimes and hunted up a dime machine. Pretty soon the five dimes were gone. "Well," said she philosophically, "easy come, easy go."

That ended our gambling.

About eight o'clock we worked our way back to the dining room. The door was closed. Nobody was being admitted.

"What's up?" I asked the door keeper.

"Floor show on now. Doors won't be open again till nine o'clock."

"What number is up then?" I asked.

"Hundred and three," said he.

That was quite a ways short of 163. And Shirley and I were hungry. Giving our tickets to a young couple who had just arrived, we started out to find a place to eat.

We drove along the wide, brilliantly lighted boulevard, looking at the palatial buildings that line both sides of the street for mile upon mile. Liveried chauffeurs and majordomos were helping expensively dressed men and women out of expensive-looking cars and into the foyers of expensive-looking buildings.

"Let's go back to the trailer and get something to eat," said Shirley.

"Not on your life," I said. "We're going to dine out. You pick the place."

Just then we passed a hamburger stand that somehow had sneaked into the line of fabulously expensive buildings.

"That's the place," said Shirley.

So we went in and got hamburgers. Thus ended our big night of gambling and carousing. But since they were pretty good hamburgers I shouldn't be surprised if we *did* get the best meal in town for the money.

Next day at the California border where we had to stop for agricultural inspection, the inspector was an amiable sort. He seemed to enjoy looking through our sleek trailer.

"Nice job you've got here," he said.

I agreed that it was a nice job. Then Shirley, emboldened by his friendliness, ventured.

"It almost broke our hearts not to bring home some of Utah's beautiful fruit."

"Why didn't you?" he asked.

"Why didn't we!" Shirley echoed. "Because we knew you'd take it way from us, that's why."

She was remembering with what distress we had given up a bushel of big juicy Bartlett pears right here at this station a number of years back.

"What in particular did you want to bring?" inquired the inspector.

"Oh, pears, melons, things like that."

"You can bring in all the Utah melons and pears you want to," said the inspector. "That ban was lifted a long time ago."

We thought nostalgically of the great baskets piled high with fruit and vegetables at the roadside in front of Utah farms, with big luscious melons priced at ten cents apiece. But it was too late to do anything about it.

Before heading for our home in the desert we stopped in Los Angeles to visit friends and relatives. Los Angeles was blanketed with smog, the worst we had ever encountered there. It made our eyes smart. But we decided to stay anyhow. So we located a trailer park and set up our temporary home for a few days of city living. That, incidentally, is how we visit friends and relatives nowadays. Thus we sleep in our own beds, which we like. And we do not discommode our hosts.

One relative, a sister, lives in Long Beach. To get there, the shortest route is by way of the Santa Ana Freeway for part of the distance. But when we got on the freeway, even without our trailer hooked on behind, the other cars whizzed past us. After our long summer in the quiet Washington countryside this traffic seemed to be moving at a simply idiotic speed. For a while we kept in the right lane. But the way cars came sweeping in from the feeder lanes on my right, I didn't feel comfortable. It seemed to me that the drivers didn't even look sideways, simply swooping into the freeway like unguided missiles. Since there were two more lanes on my left, I moved over into the middle one. The nice conservative middle way, that's for me, I thought. But I had hardly got into that lane when there came a honk behind me.

There you are, I thought disgustedly. Discourteous city drivers. He can see there's another lane to my left. Let him use that—or wait till I'm good and ready to move over.

The horn honked again, more insistent this time.

Go ahead and toot, I thought. It's *your* ulcer.

A siren began its nasty growling, right at my tail. I looked back through my mirror. Oh, oh, I thought, what have I done now? But I lost no time in getting over to the side of the road and looking for a place to stop.

"I stopped you," said the stern-faced young officer leaning on our window sill, "for violating city ordinance number five-two-five-point-one. That's traveling too slow on the freeway. You were going forty miles in a fifty-five-mile zone, and not keeping in the right lane."

The ticket cost us eleven dollars.

Well, one way and another this trip brought us more inconveniences and unpleasantness than any other of comparable length. But this I'd like to say to the gentleman in the trailer supply store: neither during the trip nor at any time since have we thought of giving up trailering. Would you throw out a bushel of delicious apples because you found some spots on one of the apples?

CHAPTER XI

TRAILER CLUBS FOR FUN AND SOCIABILITY

On a bright May morning a few years ago, Shirley and I drove to the Pomona Fairgrounds, home of the Los Angeles County Fair. May is far from fair time. We were not there to visit a fair, but to attend an *af*fair that had many of the characteristics of a fair. It had the same bustle, color, and excitement, plus a lot more fun. It was an annual gathering of TTCA, Travel Trailer Clubs of America — a national organization which exists for the purpose of promoting fun and friendships among trailerists.

We followed the winding tree-lined road past the empty exhibit buildings, past the deserted race track and grandstand, and on into the fairground's trailer park. This trailer park is maintained by the fair association for the use of exhibitors, racing people, entertainers, and park employees. At this time of year it was made available for our use. Under the large English walnut trees which furnished admirable shade, with blacktop paving, with lights, water, and sewer connections to each lot, it made an ideal site for our meeting.

The names "trailer caravan" and "travel trailer clubs" may sound a good deal alike. But as they have developed they are fairly distinct entities. Since more and more people are becoming interested in trailers and trailer traveling, it is well to understand the differences between the two types of organizations. It is one thing to own a trailer, it is something else again to know how to get the best use out of your trailer. Understanding the nature of the two types of organizations may help in this.

Not that the two are mutually exclusive. Far from it. Caravans are immensely social. And social clubs (or at least certain members of social clubs) go on caravans. Nevertheless the two have different purposes and consequently different characteristics. Here are some of the main differences:

1. MEMBERSHIP. Caravans, by and large, are open to all. That is, a certain trailer manufacturer will organize a caravan to, say, Mexico. Anyone owning that type of trailer is automatically eligible to join the caravan. Or the trailer manufacturers' association may organize a caravan to, say, Alaska, and throw the doors open to the owners of any of the trailers manufactured by the association's members. Or one of the trailer publications may organize a caravan to, well, almost anywhere. And the invitation may be to any reader of the publication, in the spirit of "Come on, join the fun!"

Membership in social clubs, in contrast, is selective. One joins by invitation. The club invites those who they believe will fit in with the spirit of the club. Sometimes the total membership in the club may be limited by the bylaws (one club has a limit of fifty members; the membership is always full with a long waiting list). In such cases the only answer is, organize another club. Usually, however, social trailer clubs welcome new members. This spirit is exemplified by one club which places the following humorous restrictions on membership:

1. You have to be alive.
2. You have to pull a trailer.
3. You have to quit being a stinker.

2. DURATION. Caravans meet on call and for a specific junket. It may be to Canada, Mexico, Europe, Africa, or, like one recent small band of trailers, behind Russia's "Iron Curtain." The whole world is being opened up for trailer caravans — which fact may conceivably have an international bearing upon inter-racial understanding. Actually, setting up housekeeping in a foreign country gives a different perspective from staying in a plush hotel; and from the standpoint of the foreign people, having our little houses set up near theirs, with the frequent exchange of visiting courtesies which always take place, they get a different concept of us than, say, the movies sometimes give.

3. AREA COVERED. Caravans draw members from all over the United States and Canada (and increasingly even from Europe).

Social clubs, because of their permanent setup, are largely limited to members of a given area.

Other differences will become apparent as we go along.

That day as Shirley and I drove into the fairgrounds trailer park we found that each club had been assigned a special section. We drove down the lane between various clubs. First we passed the North American Aviation Club (evidently not all the airplane employees want to travel by air, not all the time, anyhow); their big and gaudy banners told the world just who they were and made clear the fact that they did not intend to hide their light under a bushel. Next came a club with the enigmatic name "Ugo Shonton"; it was evidently an Indian name for they had erected a totem pole to which each arriving trailer added a section. Farther along was the "Draggin' Wagon" club from Bakersfield, California; in order that no one would mistake their identity they sported a huge cardboard dragon equipped with a device which periodically belched puffs of smoke from its flaming nostrils. Other clubs were the "IMPS" Intermountain Pals; the "Palms to Pines" from Palm Springs in the desert and Idlewild in the mountains; the "Tillicums" from Oregon; the "Happy Wanderers" from Illinois; the "Hi-De-Hos" from Idaho; and so on.

There appeared to be at least a couple of hundred trailers. Everywhere was joviality. One group, I believe it was the Long Beach Standard Oil Employees, had set up a record player and were playing square dance records and dancing in the roped-off street in front of their encampment.

Immediately apparent was one more difference between these social clubs and caravans. Everywhere were children. Rafts of children, shouting, laughing, dancing. And what was most interesting, children and adults playing and dancing together. One father said to me, "If these trailer clubs did nothing more than get our children off the city streets for a weekend now and then, they would be worthwhile. But they do so much more!" One of the "more" things evidently was getting the families out and having fun as family units.

In contrast, caravans, by their very natures, have few children — ordinarily only a small number of grandchildren whom grandpas and grandmas have brought along for the big adventure. Caravans are composed of persons who can take six or eight weeks for a trip, which means that the majority are older people either retired or semi-retired. Social trailer clubs, on the other hand, get their memberships chiefly from persons still employed, who can take only weekends or possibly two- or three-week vacations for comparatively short jaunts. These little trips provide opportunity for working fathers and busy mothers to get away from the stresses and strains of their jobs for short intervals and come back refreshed.

But the differences between the two types of organizations should not be overstressed. Some social clubs, particularly in resort areas, may be largely made up of retired persons. In these cases caravans for the group are accepted practice. For example, the members of one Palm Springs social club make annual summer tours to a salmon fishing resort in Washington. One type of organization may, indeed often does, merge into the other type. That was the case with the social trailer club Shirley and I belong to. We were attending our first TTCA meeting because members of our first big Mexican caravan who lived in the desert area had organized into a social club, and were meeting for the first time with the national association of social trailer clubs.

Likewise, although there were many young married couples with children here at this gathering, by no means were they all young. Many we encountered were our own ages. Being a retired school man I was pleased to come across some of my former school associates. One of these was the Ross Frasher mentioned earlier. Ross while still Principal of North Hollywood High School bought a small trailer and upon invitation joined the Pacific Trailer Club. He and his wife Mary became so enamored of trailering that upon retirement they moved to Palm Springs and took up residence in a spacious mobile home in one of the trailer parks. But they still kept their travel trailer and continued their association with the Pacific Club—taking frequent trips back to the Los Angeles area in order to join the club on weekend excursions. "These clubs," said Ross enthusiastically, "enable you to make friends with some of the grandest people on earth."

In the course of our further conversation Ross added another thought which deserves special emphasis in this book. He said, "What better way could one possibly find to prepare for retirement than to join one of these clubs? The Pacific Club certainly did a great deal to provide a rich and rewarding retirement for Mary and me."

One of the most interesting persons we met at the rally was the organization's president that year, Colonel Richard Hayes. Colonel Hayes, a retired Army officer, presided at the opening session from a wheel chair, but in spite of his physical handicap he radiated verve and good spirits. This dynamic individual, we learned, had endured frequent bouts with surgery, but none the less had a vitality and an out-giving quality which were captivating. All of his work for TTCA (and it had been an enormous amount, for he was one of the moving spirits in getting the national organization launched) was done for the love of the organization and what it stands for. There are no paid officials. The organization is purely non-profit.

Colonel Hayes, in reporting on the rapid growth of TTCA, said, "TTCA headquarters is flooded with inquiries like 'Is there a club in my area that I can join?' and 'How can we start a club?' and so forth." Then, after answering these and other questions, he laid himself open for more work by adding, "If you want to know anything more, write me and I'll see that you get the information."

Here and there throughout the three-day meeting we heard of short trips various clubs had enjoyed, or were in process of planning. One group from Los Angeles had gone to Velasquez Rocks, a section of weird rock formations out toward what is known as "the high desert," where many movie Westerns are shot. Another group had gone to Oak Creek Canyon in Arizona. Another to the Colorado River for a weekend of fishing. Another to Kern River on a similar mission. A number of clubs had joined in a trip to Hemet and the Ramona Pageant. One club had staged a trip into a section of the country especially interesting to its "rock-hound" members; and another club had staged a similar trip for its "bird-watchers." In the process of incubating were trips to the Portland Rose Festival, a strawberry festival somewhere, Zion Park, Sante Fe, New Mexico, and so on and so on.

But I really think I got the best concept of the activities of a really active club by reading the monthly newsletter put out by one of the older clubs. It was being distributed, and chuckled over, by members of the club there at the assembly. I had a chance to look at it. It consisted of fourteen pages (pocket-size pages) of mimeographed material, mainly dealing with a report of the doings of various members of the club. The lead story concerned the most recent rendezvous of the club, and the report was hilarious. Evidently the entertainment committee had made a great hit with the schedule of events they had planned, and the writer of the article was in good form in reporting it. Next came a round-the-clock account of what certain small splinters of the club had been doing; and the summary seemed appropriate that "they had been scattering to the four winds." And finally came the log of activities of individual members. The So-and-sos (no insult intended) had been to Florida, the Blanks to the Middlewest, the Whoosits to Mesa Verde, Mr. and Mrs. Cameralover to the High Sierras in search of fall color shots, others to Lake Tahoe, Ojai, Yellowstone, Borrego Valley, and on and on. How the members feel toward the club was indicated by a letter from an absent member, saying in part, "We're on our way home, and looking forward to the next meeting ... How good you are all going to look to us!"

It was here at this meeting that we first heard of a project which since then has become a burgeoning program. That is, clubs buying sites in desirable locations for holding their rendezvous. Such sites, to our knowledge, are now owned by clubs in Washington, Oregon, and California. No doubt Florida has many. And other clubs throughout the country which have not yet come to this author's attention. One such project Shirley and I visited on the Colorado River. It was a plot of several acres having an excellent bit of river frontage. Here (in contrast to some other developments) individual lots were sold to club members. In addition, the entire river frontage was held for the group as a whole, as well as a community center in which had been erected a modest club room.

Altogether we found the rally to be an exhilarating experience. Not only was it pleasing to meet our own trailer friends and get acquainted with new ones, but it was heartening to find so many families of young couples with children having fun together in this simple, wholesome, outdoors way.

CHAPTER XII

THE SWEETEST WAY HOME

Assume that you are in Northeast Washington somewhere north of Spokane and want to get to Palm Springs to spend the winter — which there's no reason you shouldn't do if you're foot-loose and have a trailer. There are numerous routes you could take.

The most direct and fastest route is U.S. 395, which goes through Pendleton, Oregon, and Reno, Nevada, but in the main traverses sparsely settled country and is relatively direct; we have — on an occasion when there was some urgency — made the trip home in three and a half days over U.S. 395 (usually we take five days or more). Another possible route is U.S. 95 through Idaho's Coeur d'Alene and Salmon River country. Or you could go a bit farther east and take in Yellowstone Park, Idaho Falls, Salt Lake City, and so on to Los Angeles (this is the route I wrote about in "Trailering Troubles"). Or if you preferred you could take a route slightly *west* of U.S. 395 and travel through Central Washington, Central Oregon, and Central California by way of U.S. 99. Or you could move over a bit farther west and follow the coast line most of the way down, detouring if you felt so inclined around famous Olympic Peninsula.

During the retirement years in which we have spent our summers north of Spokane and our winters in the desert near Palm Springs, we have followed all of these routes one or more times — as well as various combinations of these routes. Each has a good deal of scenic beauty to recommend it.

But last summer, acting upon the adage that the longest way round is the sweetest way home, we took the sweetest way of all. En route to Southern California from Northeast Washington we went by way of British Columbia. If you will take a look at a map you will observe that by no stretch of the imagination could it be called a direct route.

It was in the spirit of butterflies rather than hummingbirds that we took this round-about way. Hummingbirds zoom to where they're going. Butterflies flutter and meander. Shirley and I, to be sure, are somewhat antique butterflies with our wings a bit frayed, but we still like to flutter and meander. So when we headed for our desert home we spread our wings and fluttered over a scenic route up into Canada, through the fruit orchards that border the lakes of Okanagan Valley, over part of the exciting Cariboo Trail, into some fairly wild country on a fishing excursion west of Prince George, down the Switzerlandlike Fraser River Canyon, into Vancouver B.C., and on south along the Washington-Oregon-California blue Pacific coast line. This trip carried us something over three thousand miles, instead of the zoom route which is nearer fifteen hundred miles.

A major difference between ordinary automobile traveling and trailer traveling lies in the spirit of the travelers. Travelers who want to take the shortest possible line between two points and race from one point to the other, to my way of thinking ought not to pull a trailer. They probably should travel by jet liner. Anyhow they shouldn't desecrate the wonderful spirit of trailering.

We old folk who travel in trailers, it seems to me, should be like young lovers who know that the sweetest way home is not the shortest or the quickest. *Their* object is not to whoosh somewhere as fast as possible, but to gather sweet pleasures along the way. Likewise old lovers — man and wife who, as Bobby Burns puts it, are tottering down the hill together — should be in no hurry to get anywhere. Their object should be to capture every last "smidgin" of pleasure as they go along, sip every last drop of sweetness of the flowers that border the way.

Anyhow that is the spirit in which Shirley and I do our trailer traveling, and the spirit in which we took this sweetest way home.

As I sit here reliving and re-enjoying the leisurely trip I think of that first night we spent north of the border. All afternoon we had been driving through first Washington's Okanagan Valley and then Canada's Okanagan Valley. The apple, peach, and pear trees were so laden with fruit that every tree had to be braced, many with twenty or more props. So it was not surprising when we pulled into Worth's Trailer Park in Okanagan Falls to find it situated in a fruit orchard.

Mr. Worth helped me hook up the utilities, then straightening said, "You see all the fruit," with a sweeping gesture that took in the heavily laden peach and pear trees all around us. "Help yourselves."

"You mean," gasped Shirley, "for free?" There was an upward sweep of incredulity on the word *free*.

"Help yourselves," repeated Mr. Worth. "We're not marketing the fruit this year. See that stove," pointing to a wood stove with a big boiler on top and a pile of stove wood next to the stove, "that's for any of you who like to do canning. We don't like to see the fruit go to waste."

"What's the matter?" I inquired. "Market off?"

"That's part of the trouble," he replied, "but also there's some quality of the fruit this year that makes it hard to keep. Has to be harvested right on the dot, and of course we can't do that. So . . ." he shrugged, "use all you want."

He appeared to be taking the loss philosophically, possibly because he had another source of income in the trailer park. But it was a striking example of the tribulations and uncertainties our farmer friends have to face.

Whatever was wrong with the marketability of the fruit did not affect its looks or its taste. The great luscious peaches — one of them would practically fill your hand — were the kind that make you smack your lips in gustatory rapture. We didn't can any, because we already had canned all the Washington fruit we could conveniently carry in our trailer. But we did eat piggishly. And we did load up with a generous supply of the big pink-cheeked peaches and the big juicy pears, enough to last us many days. They kept well enough in our refrigerator.

Penticton, our next stop, is strategically situated on a narrow strip of land between Okanagan Lake and Skaha Lake. Boating, swimming, fishing, and smart shops lure visitors from far distances. Shirley succumbed to the smart shops and I to the fishing.

Our lunch that day was on a paved turn-off overlooking seventy-mile-long Okanagan Lake. There I tried to do something which I have attempted many times before, that is to take a color picture through the trailer's open doorway. But this picture, like others similarly taken, turned out pretty flat. It showed the door frame and a spot of blue outside, but the charm of the view wasn't there at all. I'd like to have a collection of pictures of the scenic picnic spots we've enjoyed on our travels, but it would take a better photographer than I am to do justice to the scenes we see through our trailer windows and open door.

One interesting feature of this trip was that our 1954 trailer caravan had come right through this district. We were now having a good chance to compare the two types of trailer travel. People sometimes ask us, "Which do you prefer, going with a caravan or by yourselves?" We have only one answer, "We prefer both." We don't want to be deprived of either. Caravans are more strenuous, but they're also more exhilarating. They're something special. You can't duplicate them in any other form of entertainment that we know. But for a steady diet, caravans are pretty spicy food. Quiet, relaxing, butterfly-like trips such as we were now taking are more soothing to the nervous system and more stimulating to the digestion.

At Vernon I looked up a businessman I had met when we were there on the caravan. He had taken several of us on a highly sucessful trout-fishing trip. Naturally I didn't want to pass through town without paying my respects and again expressing my appreciation. And if in the back of my mind was the thought that he might repeat — I wasn't disappointed.

"You came right by Woods Lake on your way up here," he said. "That's where I keep my boat. If you don't mind driving back the few miles, I'll meet you there tomorrow morning. There's a good trailer park there."

In our meandering mood driving back a few miles meant nothing. So we turned around. Then our friend had another thought. He hurried into the street to intercept us.

"Say," he said, "you might like to do some fishing this evening. I'll call the storekeeper — he has the boat dock too — and tell him to let you have the boat."

The many instances of such generous friendliness, both when we were with caravans and when we were by ourselves, have made me proud of the Scotch-Irish-English-Canadian blood that makes up my American blood stream.

On our way back to Woods Lake we took time out to stop for a few minutes at another lake along the route, the so-called lake of many colors — Lake Kalamalka. From a view point high above the lake we saw the patches of iridescent colors play over the lake's surface. Among all the rainbow hues the color which impressed me most was an odd combination of opalescent green, blue, and purple which seemed to move back and forth over the water. Where the water found that color to reflect from the skies I could not imagine.

Incidentally, at these view points Canada has a unique system for taking care of litter. Big, gaudily painted creatures with bulging eyes and huge mouths look as if they might have dropped from some fantastic land of make-believe. But their purpose is made evident by a sign on the hinged upper lip above the mouth, "Feed me." The method is effective. One sees few cans, bottles, and paper tissues along the roads.

The fish we caught at Woods Lake were a species of landlocked salmon called kokanee. Their deep pink flesh is remarkably tender and tasty. In fact, if there is any better tasting fish to be found I'd like to know where so I can go and get some.

At Kelowna, an attractive small city on the bank of Okanagan Lake, we had a pleasant recollection of the entertainment accorded the caravan when we were there. Members of the yacht club took us on a boat ride on the lake, following which we were entertained at a green corn roast around a huge bonfire. This time, traveling alone, we received no such hospitality. Nor did the mayor and other city officials meet us at the edge of town and escort us down Main Street in state. Our passing through didn't stir up a ripple. That's one thing about a caravan, everyone knows you're in town.

Kamloops is not only the home of the famous Kamloops trout, it is a thriving and fast-growing city. We had lunch at the hotel where the caravan had been entertained at a haggis dinner. Haggis has certain patriotic and romantic associations for Scotchmen. Our banquet that night was presented to the accompaniment of colorful ceremonies including candles, kilts, and bagpipes, also huge silver trays and serving dishes, and a Bobby Burns poem paying tribute to haggis — and of course the haggis. But Shirley and I did not order haggis this time. To be truthful, haggis is one Scotch item we can do without. One of my choicest pictures was one taken that night, just as a portion of the pudding — it is made of the giblets of a calf or a sheep — was being served to one of the caravaners, and he was looking sidewise down his nose at the concoction just as the flash went off. Shirley and I, feeling toward the pudding the way he looked, had no trouble at all passing it up this time. But we had no such feeling toward the dinner of Kamloops trout the Kamloops Chamber of Commerce served the caravan in the city park. Driving a well-equipped kitchen atop a truck into the park where we were bivouacked, they cooked and served us generous portions of the savory fish. This time we would have appreciated another go at a feast like that. But nobody offered it to us.

Upon leaving Kamloops we parted from the route the caravan had taken. Wanting to see more of this interesting country we drove on west and north. For many miles we followed the Thompson River, a clear cold stream looking exactly as a good fishing stream should look.

Cache Creek is the junction of the eastern and western Alcan routes. Note, *routes*; not Highways. The actual Alcan Highway begins at Dawson Creek a few hundred miles farther north. But Cache Creek is on the route, and it like the other towns and cities along the way is profiting from the greatly augmented Alaskan travel these days. Cache Creek probably has a population of only a few hundred persons, but it has wide streets, good stores and restaurants, and a general air of prosperity.

Here we did what we later decided was a rather foolish thing. We parted temporarily from our trailer. By pre-arrangement we met a Washington couple who live near our summer Shangri-La. With them we went up the storied Cariboo Trail to Prince George, westward along the Prince Rupert road as far as Burns Lake, southward some fifty miles to the northeast corner of Tweedsmuir Provincial Park. Don't let the name "park" deceive you into visions of green lawns and manicured shrubs. This is frontier country, thinly populated. Canada has the far-sighted policy of setting aside huge tracts of land for later development as the country develops. Tweedsmuir is one of these tracts. Between Burns Lake and our destination we saw the effects of the activities of the Kitimat Aluminum Company several hundred miles farther west. At one point the backed-up water in Lake Ootsa had overflowed and cut its own wide channel through the forest for sixty miles. Our destination was Bear Lake, a small body of water beyond Ootsa Lake. Our Washington friends had been extended the use of a cabin on Bear Lake. Here in this scenically wild country we stayed and fished for four days — enough time to give us all the fish we could eat and wanted to take home. Of the dozens of rainbow trout we caught the smallest was fifteen inches.

We smoked what we could not eat and carried them with us when we left. We also carried away with us the memory of some of nature's grandeur, and the haunting sound of a loon's call at twilight.

This little side excursion, from Cache Creek and back again, according to Shirley's log took us exactly one thousand and twelve miles. Three nights' lodging going and coming cost $21.50 for each couple. With our trailer it would have cost not more than $6. Besides, instead of eating in restaurants we would have eaten in the trailer, at least most of the time, thereby saving many more dollars. That is why we felt that we made a mistake in not taking the trailer, even though the use of the cabin was complimentary. And another "besides," being creatures of habit we would have slept better in our own beds in the trailer.

Back at Cache Creek, the Thompson River with the sun shining on its riffles seemed to smile a welcome. And, since at this point the river turned south, we were glad to follow it again. At Lytton the Thompson plunges frothily into the Fraser River, and together they go churning and roaring down the Fraser Canyon. There were times, as we followed along the steep canyon walls and got occasional glimpses down into roaring chasms, that we felt it would not be too hard to follow the Thompson River's example and tumble into the Fraser. Actually, though, this newly widened and improved highway is well engineered and comparatively safe. All one has to do is avoid letting the gorgeous scenery distract him from the business of driving. The grades are not unduly steep nor is the roadbed narrow. And the dramatic landscape is worth going far to see. We were glad that we had not let a well-meaning but timid autoist discourage us from taking the trip with a trailer, as he had tried to do. It reminded me of what I had heard an old caravaner say in a caravan "bull session." "If I had been bluffed out by all the discouraging advice I've had about roads, I'd never have gone much of anywhere."

At Spences Bridge I was glad that the park proprietor helped me hook up the utilities. Some do and some don't. I particularly appreciated this help because of an approaching storm. Big sprinkles struck us before we finished hooking up. And I had hardly got inside before a thunder-crashing rain was pelting down on the trailer. There, to the fortissimo music of raindrops playing tunes on our aluminum roof, we ate the last of those wonderful peaches that had lasted all the way from Okanagan Falls.

Vancouver is as colorful and distinctive as any city has a right to be. But cities are not our special dish. So, after only a couple of days there, we were glad to be back on the open road once more.

Of the long, scenic journey down the coast I have neither space nor inclination to write, except for a couple of incidents that we found of special interest.

Stopping for a short visit with our long-time friend Harold

Fischer, manager of the trout hatchery at Aberdeen, Washington, we
were fascinated in watching some of Harold's activities in fish culture,
and in hearing his accounts of fish habits and instincts. The hatchery
concentrates upon the rearing of steelhead trout. Unlike other members of the large rainbow family, steelhead are ocean-going. Almost indistinguishable from other members of the family in external
appearance, especially in their early months of life, some inborn
instinct makes them quite different in nature. It compels them to go
downstream to the ocean, and likewise it compels them to go back
up the same stream when their spawning time comes. If, said Harold,
one of them on its way upstream is taken from that stream and placed
in another stream, instead of going on up it will turn back and return
to the ocean, seek its own "childhood" stream once more and keep
going up until it comes to the place from which it started the trip to
the ocean in the first place. Strange and powerful influences, these
animal instincts!

On the coast west of Aberdeen the enormous wild blackberry vines
hang thick with large berries and the vines are to be found on
practically every fence and overflowing into the surrounding fields.
From these berries Shirley makes a jelly which must be on the
menus of all the gods of that region, for it tastes like ambrosia is
supposed to taste. So naturally we went blackberrying. While we
were busily engaged at our task, with my pail nearly full of berries
I started to move from one location to another. As I left the fence
and moved back to the road, a creeping vine lovingly encircled my
ankle. In seeking to break its embrace I stumbled and started to fall.
Then, striving to regain my balance without spilling the berries, my
body started to turn. Then to whirl. And in a sort of whirling dervish
action I gyrated across the road — and sat down in my pail of berries.
I survived the ordeal but my pants didn't. The stain never came out.

On the last leg of our homeward journey we took another side
trip, this time into Paradise — Paradise, California, that is. Trailer
friends having extolled the town as the perfect retirement spot, we
stopped to investigate. Located in the foothills out of Chico, it is an
area of striking contrasts. Flat benches give place here and there to
deep, steep-walled canyons. Through one of the deep canyons not
far distant flows lovely Feather River. Extensive apple orchards have
been carved from the tall pines and broad-flung oaks that cover the
benches. Farm, city, and mountains seem to have joined hands to
create a unique resort community. Although the elevation is only
twelve to fifteen hundred feet, it has something of the air of a mountain village. We got a hookup in one of the several modern trailer
parks and stayed a few days to enjoy the apple harvesting and to buy
a box of the savory fruit. It was not hard to see why some retirees
find this area to be their personal retirement paradise. It did not,

however, lure us away from our Washington and California-desert combination.

But now we were happy to be getting home. In some respects Shirley and I are like those steelhead. Although passionately fond of travel, especially our particular kind of travel, we still want at times to get into the stream (of traffic) that leads *home*. And that home, we have found, may be either a conventional house or one of the commodious mobile homes parked in one of the luxurious trailer parks in which we have lived. One may be as richly endowed as the other with all the sentiment we attach to the magic word *home*. Indeed, at times we feel that our little traveling trailer is as truly *home* as any other home. Nevertheless we still like a home base.

So long as we have the home base waiting for us, we're usually in no great hurry to get there. Often, as on this trip, we take a long round-about way to get there.

Two lovely television girls, twins, are singing the advice these days that we should double our pleasure, double our fun, by chewing Doublemint gum. On this trip in which we traveled over three thousand miles on the way home instead of the fifteen hundred miles of the zoom route, we found a better way to double our pleasure, double our fun — by doubling the distance traveled, making it "the sweetest way home."